REAL MEN DON'T WRITE COLUMNS

REAL MEN DON'T WRITE COLUMNS

A Psychologist's Humorous Look at
Men, Women, Family, and
Psychotherapy

Mark Sherman

A collection of 36 of his *Huguenot
Herald* and *New Paltz Times*
columns (1985-2003)

Published by the author
in New Paltz, New York
2004

REAL MEN DON'T WRITE COLUMNS
A Psychologist's Humorous Look at Men, Women, Family, and Psychotherapy

by Mark Sherman

Published by the author

Copyright ©2004 by Mark A. Sherman

All of these columns first appeared in *The New Paltz Times* or one of its predecessors. They are reprinted by permission of the publisher, Ulster Publishing.

ISBN 0-9742917-0-6

Mark Sherman
PO Box 206
New Paltz, NY 12561

website: www.ProfMarkSherman.com

For Shelley

CONTENTS

Preface

For nearly two decades, I have written a bi-weekly humor column for a local weekly paper in the quirky college town of New Paltz, New York (a mere 25 miles from the slightly more famous and perhaps even quirkier Woodstock). The paper's name has changed several times during that span and is now the *New Paltz Times*. I realize that this puts me one word away from fame and fortune.

The 460 or so pieces I've written over these years cover a wide variety of fun-filled topics ranging from Lyme disease to hernia surgery, from global warming to the possibility of an asteroid hitting the earth. One column answered the age-old question of why there are more bar fights than diner fights.

But you won't find those in here. Since my day job for many years was teaching psychology at the State University of New York at New Paltz, reading, research, and teaching in psychology – with an emphasis on gender issues – took up much of my time. The rest of my time was spent with my wife and children, or fruitlessly trying to achieve more than a modicum of mental health. Thus, in this collection I have chosen to limit myself to the topics I know best: men, women, family, and psychotherapy.

From "Solving the Parent Problem," originally published in 1985, to "True Intimacy" in 2003, I have covered many, if not all, of the major personal issues faced by men, women, and children in America today.

In pieces like "Free Association" (1994) and "Ready to Fly Solo" (1997), I make affectionate fun of my own as yet unsuccessful search -- one I know I share with millions of others -- for something approaching a normal life.

The columns in this collection appear in chronological order and cover a period of nearly 18 years. Readers who start with the first one -- which, along with all the others, has its date of original publication at the end -- and read through will, depending on their point of view, see the author maturing with age or deteriorating.

Though I wrote all these pieces with humor, there may very well be some practical and helpful suggestions nestled in them. After all, being a psychologist probably influences everything I write. And I hope you don't dismiss my ideas just because they seem outlandish; in my work, I have found that some of my ideas which seemed bizarre one year are all the rage a year, or ten, or fifty years later. Who knows but that my modest proposals in "Solving the Parent Problem" and "Time for a Speak-Out" may someday turn into reality. Of course, someone else will realize fame and fortune from this -- perhaps even one of my readers. If so, I would appreciate at least an acknowledgment or thank you note (and a little cash wouldn't hurt).

I wish to thank many people for their encouragement and support, and do so on the following two pages. But my most heartfelt thanks go to my wife Shelley. She is my "quality control." If she doesn't laugh at what I've written, I try again -- after an appropriate period of pouting and sulking, of course.

Acknowledgments

When you write an acknowledgments page, you're almost begging for resentments from others and guilt feelings for yourself, because you're sure to forget someone, and probably someone important. So I will say right now that if you don't see your name here, it's either because you did nothing at all to help me or I forgot you.

That said, I would like to thank:

Phoebe Prosky, who, when I said I wrote all the time, said, "Why don't you write a column?"

Jeremiah Horrigan, who suggested I send pieces to his publisher

Geddy Sveikauskas, publisher of the *New Paltz Times* and its predecessors (where all these pieces first appeared) – not only for publishing them but for giving full permission for me to publish them elsewhere

Julie O'Corozine, Debbie Alexsa, and other *N.P. Times* editors and staff

Readers of my column, who often (but never often enough, of course) have told me how much they enjoy it

Lina Lynch and others at PDQ who were so helpful in the printing of this book

For their help, inspiration, and encouragement: Kim Blisard, Mary Davidson, the late Mary Drew, Caren Fairweather, Jon Fackler, Steve Lewis, Fed Poole, my wonderful writing group (Lyn, Bonnie, Wendy, Jody, Kala, Carol, and Nancy), Linda Gluck, Lauren Thomas, Lavon Morris-Grant, S. Sapyta, D. Ambrose, Margaret Lobenstine, George Miller, Gail Kuenstler, Manny Strauss, Sarah Gardner, David Morse, Michael Gold, and several unnamed mental health professionals.

Special friends Peter O'Brien, Marshall Rafal, Steve Ruelke, Dean Scher, and many (well, at least a few) others

With love and gratitude, my family: my wonderful wife, Shelley, who is the always the first (and sometimes the last) person to read everything I write, whose suggestions are incredibly helpful, whose own sense of humor is terrific, and who is simply my anchor; my three beautiful boys and my two beautiful daughters-in-law; my brother, Carl, who's a terrific writer himself and who is almost as funny as I am

My late parents, Milton and Estelle Sherman, who appreciated and encouraged my writing, and virtually guaranteed that I'd have to grow up with a sense of humor.

Solving The Parent Problem

How can a nation which has sent people to the moon not know how to deal with its aging parents? Why is it that otherwise competent adult human beings become totally immobilized and confused when trying to get along with their parents? More importantly, what can we do to solve the problem? Is it even possible to solve it, to make everyone happy, our parents and ourselves?

I think a major part of the problem is the geographical distance between many of us and our parents. Back when I was a kid, everyone lived close to parents. We were two blocks from my paternal grandmother; at three miles, we were relatively far from my maternal grandparents. But look at now. If your parents live 85 miles away, they are close. Many of our parents live at least a thousand miles away.

So the whole system of interaction has changed. This is especially true as regards visits. I saw my grandparents a lot – several times a week. The visits were short, often including a meal, which was generally delicious. Then, after a few hours, the visit was over and the visitors would go home. But if your parents live 85

1

or 1000 miles away, you cannot easily do this. Depending on the distance between you, visits can last anywhere from overnight to several weeks.

This is where the problems begin. The visit goes just fine at first, but after several hours, just when in the old days someone would be going home, you are still together. Tension begins and rises, and, after several days, chaos may occur. Worst of all, you may start to hate your parent or parents, and though they won't admit it, they may be getting to hate you.

But have you ever noticed that no matter how terrible someone's parents sound when described by their adult child, they are almost invariably interesting, charming, polite and pleasant when you meet them? And have you noticed that when you introduce your totally impossible mother or father to a friend, the friend finds your parent terrific?

Probably that judgment – "terrific" – is much closer to the truth. Objectively, the vast majority of our parents *are* interesting, intelligent, warm and polite. So why do we torture ourselves and our parents needlessly? Why do we have to spend so much time with our *own* parents? Why don't we start a Parent Exchange Program?

In such a program, your parents would – at least from time to time – stay with your friends, and their parents would stay with you. Think about it. Instead of spending a long week-end or longer with someone whom you are pretty convinced has ruined your life, you would spend it with one or two people who are interesting, witty, interested in you, etc.

Look at it from your parents' point of view. Instead of being with young, ungrateful people – no picnic, as Shakespeare makes clear in his famous line, "How sharper than a serpent's tooth it is to have a thankless child" – they would be with people interested in them, eager to hear their view of the world, appreciating their intelligence, etc. You'd be putting a little PEP in your and their lives.

After several exchange visits of this sort, your friends will probably rave to you about how great your parents are. At first you may be annoyed. After all, your friends didn't have to go through *your* childhood. These wonderful older people they tell you about didn't yell at *them* when they came home with a less than perfect report card. They didn't give *them* a curfew an hour earlier than everyone else's. They didn't object to every boy or girlfriend *they* ever went out with.

Still, after hearing all this praise of your folks, you may finally start to feel differently about them and warmly invite them to come visit you. And you may, you just may, see them in a new light, as the interesting people they really are.

At least for the first few hours of the visit.

[4/18/85]

3

Are We There Yet?

My youngest child became five years old today, an event which has led me to lots of thoughts, among which is to try to imagine what it's like to be a young child. As I think about it, I realize that it's not all birthday cakes and He-Man guys.

We were all children once, so go back with me now to that world of childhood, the world we so often yearn for. First of all, you are now short. Very short. Until you are four or five, people sometimes trip over you. And you can't reach anything. Sure you can, if you climb, but why do *you* have to be the one who always has to carry a chair over to reach the sink? Why don't houses have lower sinks? And the toilet. It's a peril! You could fall in. Really.

People are always touching you too, especially patting you on the head. They're obsessed with your hair – "Oh, it's so curly!" "Look at that red hair!" "It's so blond," or "It's so thick," or "It grows so fast." And what are you supposed to say? Thank you? Thank you for telling me I have curly hair?

And you keep hearing the word *cute*. No matter how sophisticated you try to sound, that's the only word they use – cute. On a trip that really does seem to be taking forever, you ask the perfectly reasonable question, "Are we there yet?" Everyone laughs and says you're cute.

Or say one morning you decide to tell about the dream you had last night. It's hard for you. You try to use long sentences, and it's hard. You say, "I dreamed there was a monster...and he chased me...and...I ran away..and.." You struggle for minutes to pour out your tale of fear, and at the end Dad says to Mom, "He's so cute!" Suppose Mom or Dad went to a therapist and described a dream. Do you think at the end the therapist would say, "You're so cute"?

You have no freedom either. Freedom of speech? Are you kidding? Speak your mind as an adult and people commend you for being assertive. Do it as a child and they threaten to make you eat soap. Freedom of religion? When was the last time you heard of a five-year-old who independently converted to a different religion? You even have to ask permission to go outside. You have to go to bed earlier than you want to, and then, to add insult to injury, your parents are surprised when you get up early in the morning and annoyed with you for waking them!

And there are so many minor indignities. If Mom or Dad is cold, *you* have to put a sweater on. If you feel a little under the weather, someone is sure to touch your forehead or kiss it, and if they suspect you have a fever, they may decide to, shudder, take your temperature. And you know what *that* means.

Also, sooner or later, now matter how careful you are, you'll spill your milk. At least when you do that, they won't call it cute.

And what about being picked up? I don't mean when Mom or Dad gets you at nursery school. I mean you're standing there, minding your own business, when suddenly some grown-up puts his or her hands under your arms and lifts you up in the air. I have a very strong friend who does that to me, and much as I love this guy, I'm not crazy about being picked up that way. But when you're a little kid, this happens all the time. Even heavyweight champions had to go through it when they were little.

One of the biggest insults is that the word that defines you (child) is used as an epithet by adults. Does Mom ever think of *your* feelings when she tells Dad he's acting like a child, as if it were some kind of crime? When one of your friends is annoying you, do you accuse him or her of acting like a grown-up?

No, it's an adult word out there, as any four-year-old boy who has ever tried to use a men's room knows. You can't see out of car windows. You're too short to eat over your plate, but they yell at you when you spill food in your lap. They can use words that you're not allowed to use. And they can yell at you, but you're not allowed to yell at them.

It's so difficult for you that eventually, after much soul-searching, you may decide that being a child isn't so great and that you'd rather be a grown-up. This is not an easy decision to come to, especially when you're four or five, and it's one that you feel reluctant to make public. Of course, when you do, when you blurt it out, when you say, "I want to be a grown-up!" you know what happens. They all laugh. And they say you're cute.

[1/23/86]

Party Time

Tomorrow is my youngest son's birthday party. He just turned seven. As my wife said just the other day, seven is the last cute age, at least for boys. Indeed, I will never forget a visit to a friend's house when I was about 14. His brother kept pestering us and bothering us, and my friend explained his behavior succinctly.

"He's eight," he said, and that said it all.

The problem is that since seven is borderline, a group of 7-year–olds (or even 6- and 7-year-olds, as tomorrow's party will have) can easily, at any moment, go from cute to impossible. I know this from recent experience with my middle son. I have some audio tapes from some of his early parties. At his fifth, cuteness reigns supreme. By seven, the kids are starting to outdo each other in silliness. By eight, silly has become disgusting. I don't have a tape of that, but I remember it. Anything having to do with bodily functions was a cause for hilarity.

It's not clear whether the parties became less charming because of age or the growing lack of a female influence. I had seen the proportion of girls diminish over the years, from half at age five to none at eight.

Even in today's world, with its blurring of sex roles, I don't think outright grossness is considered the height of achievement among 8-year-old girls.

I'm evading the issue at hand. In less than 24 hours our house will contain eight boys intent on fun. And we haven't planned anything yet or even asked for back-up.

You have to plan these parties. Maybe in a place like New York City, parents hire a professional – typically an unemployed and bitter actor or comedian – to dress as a clown and entertain the kids. But here in my little town, the tradition is to do it yourself; and that takes planning. You always have to plan more activities than there is time for, because some, if not all, of your ideas are going to bomb.

There was something at my son's last party that went over well. It was a little song, where the kids filled in the numbers from one to ten. As I recall, they really enjoyed it, and it took up a full five minutes of the seemingly interminable two hours. (That's another bizarre aspect of these parties. The party starts at noon. You greet the kids, beg their parents to stay, play Simon Says and Pin the Tail on the Donkey, serve the cake, and look at the clock. It's only 12:20!)

So I was heartened when, a couple of days ago, my son mentioned the song. "Daddy, remember that little song you sang at my party last year, with the numbers?"

"Yes," I said, eagerly.

"Well, don't do it this time. It's too babyish."

One of the nice things about that song was that the kids participated together. It was only mildly competitive. Many party activities are actually highly competitive, leaving some young guests with lingering doubts about their abilities.

Who invented these games? I think the Nazis invented Simon Says, a strange game in which following orders to the letter is the key to winning. The creative child, the free spirit, the dreamer always does poorly at Simon Says, and winds up wondering what's wrong with him. For such children, each game probably translates into six months of psychotherapy later.

Perhaps even crueler is Pin the Tail on the Donkey. Here is a game in which children giggle hysterically as some poor child, terrified at being blindfolded, stumbles about the house and eventually pins the tail on the floor.

And, finally, there are the gifts. No one knows the best gift to get. Your child will not be able to hide his or her disappointment at the inferior ones, and while you may be able to do so ("Oh, that's wonderful, Ryan! A pack of baseball cards!"), you won't be able to hide your feelings from the young guest's parents, who *used* to be your friends.

Even worse is when a child gives a gift way out of proportion. Your child may be delighted that Eric gave him a VCR, but you'll be alarmed. Clearly this is an attempt to buy your child's friendship, but how do you handle it?

However, eventually the party will be over. The house will quiet down, and your child will play with his new toys. And you'll thank God that there was no blood. It was a good party.

[1/21/88]

Marriage

Recently, a young woman told me about a friend who just got married.

"I'm pretty sure it's not going to work out," she said. "Both people are very impulsive and they come from very different backgrounds." "But," she added, "does that really matter? Does marriage have to be a lifetime commitment? Why not say, 'Let's see if we can make this last five years?'"

Having been married nearly 20 years, I tried to convince her that a lifetime commitment was a good thing. I found it hard. I believe that it is, but it's one of those spiritual truths that are difficult to explain in rational terms. Marriage is like the weather. Sometimes it's beautiful and sometimes it's not. But you certainly wouldn't want to do without it.

As with everything else in life, there are ways to make marriage work. There are a number of simple rules to follow that will practically guarantee that your marriage will last as long as you do.

First, most important, and something to

remember at all times: *Don't say the first thing that pops into your head.* The trouble with most marriages is that people think it means you should be spontaneous. This is absurd. How often in life does being spontaneous help you? A much better way to think of marriage is as a permanent job interview.

Of course, there are exceptions. If the first thing that pops into your head is "I love you" or "You look terrific," then by all means say it. Incidentally, with respect to physical appearance, I have discovered that women are particularly sensitive about their hair. If your wife has had her hair cut or has had a permanent, *never* say something like "I guess it will look okay when it grows in" or "Maybe it will look better after the first washing." Just say you love it.

In fact, if I know I won't be home when my wife is coming in from the hairdresser, I leave a note on the refrigerator door which says, "Your hair looks great!"

Men are not nearly so sensitive about their hair, except for the amount of it. The wife who says things like "Hey, gettin' a little bald spot up there, huh?" is probably asking for trouble. Every man knows how good it feels to have his wife run her fingers through his hair, but this good feeling is ruined when she says, "Honey, I just love running my fingers through your scalp."

Another rule of marriage is *Don't criticize your in-laws.* This may be difficult if your spouse is upset about his or her parents. You may feel that it is a sign of

13

loyalty to jump in. But don't, because if you do, you may find that the attack is now directed at you.

"My mother is driving me crazy," your wife may say. "Doesn't she know I'm a grown woman now?! I know how to raise my children!"

It may seem only natural for you to plunge in with "You're right. She's impossible. She's unhappy with her own life, and she's just taking it out on you."

Your wife's reaction to this will probably be something like "How dare you criticize my mother! Your mother is completely impossible and do I say anything about her?"

"My mother?!" you now exclaim.

You see what's happened? Your mother-in-law is now off the hook, and you and your mother are in big trouble. The best approach when your spouse criticizes a parent is to say nothing and wash the dishes, or go out and buy groceries.

As difficult an issue as parents can be for a couple, even more stressful are children. Here there is one very important rule: Don't disagree about childrearing in front of the child you are rearing. If your spouse uses punishment you think is a little too strong, such as grounding your teen-age son for a year because he didn't clean his room once, don't argue about it in front of your son. Discuss it quietly with your spouse when the two of you are alone.

The reason for this is simple. The relationship

between parents and children can best be described as war; and in war you look for an ally. What better ally can a child have than his parent? So if you argue in front of your child, he will pick whomever seems to be on his side and join in to pressure the other parent. The result is what is commonly known as chaos.

Another problem area is money. One of you wants to spend it, the other wants to save it. Here the rule is simple: *Make more of it!*

But perhaps the biggest difficulty facing a married couple is basic differences in style. One of you is calm, the other is crazed. One of you likes jazz, the other likes classical music. One likes asparagus, the other hates it. How can you deal with these differences?

Lord, I wish I knew.

[11/9/89]

15

Sherman's Shrink Speaks

Although it is considered highly unethical for a mental health professional to talk about any of his patients, Dr. Sigmund Frodsky, a psychiatrist, recently consented to be interviewed concerning one of his best-known patients, Mark Sherman. In this *Herald* exclusive, Dr. Frodsky has helped to give some insights into Sherman's bizarreness.

Herald: Dr. Frodsky, why are you doing this? Aren't you aware that the first principle of the doctor-patient relationship is confidentiality? Aren't you risking suspension of your license?

Dr. Frodsky: License? What license? I was suspended years ago for making sexual advances with patients. However, no such thing happened with Sherman. And, by the way, where is that deadbeat? He still owes me for six sessions.

Herald: How long has Sherman been seeing you?

Dr. Frodsky: Too long. Or not long enough. I mean, it has been 18 years now, sometimes as often as 16 times a week. And yet there are neuroses that are still not under control.

Herald: Such as?

Dr. Frodsky: He is very compulsive. Sometimes he has

to check a door eight or nine times to make sure it's locked. And we're talking about a closet door that doesn't even have a lock. Also, Sherman feels that he has to call his sister at least once a week.

Herald: That doesn't sound so strange.

Dr. Frodsky: Well it is, because he doesn't have a sister.

Herald: Where do you think these problems come from?

Dr. Frodsky: I think they all come from his childhood. Where else? You don't develop neuroses because you read about them on the back of a cereal box.

Herald: Could you tell us a little about his childhood?

Dr. Frodsky: Ah, that could be a whole book. Where would I begin? For a while, Sherman was the apple of his mother's eye. Unfortunately, his mother was allergic to apples, and she proceeded to break into hives whenever her little boy sat on her lap. This led Sherman to feelings of guilt, which he still carries to this day. He also carries around a marble and a 1956 baseball card. The man is really a mental case.

Herald: What about his father? How was his relationship with his father?

Dr. Frodsky: He tells me that he and his father got along well, but I'm not sure. He goes on and on about how his father took him to baseball games; but if his father's seat was behind first base, he made Mark sit behind third base. He says to me, "But it could have been worse. He could have made me sit in the bleachers." But my feeling is that this is a desperate cry for acceptance.

Herald: Is his father still living?

Dr. Frodsky: Unfortunately, no. And his last words apparently were, "Tell that kid that next time we go the game, he sits in right field." This has not been easy for Sherman to deal with.

Herald: Did Sherman have problems in school?

Dr. Frodsky: That's like asking if the Confederacy had trouble with Lincoln. Sherman never felt fully at home at school, but paradoxically, he felt very much at school when he was at home. However, from an early age it was clear that he was what teachers euphemistically call a "troublemaker."

Herald: Any examples?

Dr. Frodsky: Though he was a good reader, in the third grade he refused to read for a month. Then, when he did read, he insisted on keeping the book upside down. And he simply refused to do long division. He told me that he always considered school to be silly and that it had very little to do with the real world. So I told him, oh yeah, where would I be without all my years of schooling? To which he replied, "See what I mean?" I tell you, the man is impossible.

Herald: What is Sherman's most serious problem?

Dr. Frodsky: His clothes. The man has absolutely no taste in clothes. He wears brown pants with a blue shirt. And his belts never match his tie.

Herald: Anything else?

Dr. Frodsky: Yes. Sherman is very worried that someday

he is going to die. I keep reassuring him, but he still worries.

Herald: But he is going to die. We all are. Even you.

Dr. Frodsky: What? Me? It can't happen. I eat only carrots and broccoli, I never drive, and I don't smoke. There is no way in the world that I'm going to die.

Herald: Okay, let's change the subject. What kind of progress has Sherman made in the years you have been treating him?

Dr. Frodsky: To be honest, not much. It's true he pays his bills more quickly, but not quickly enough. Also, he's a man filled with guilt. I keep telling him that if he paid my bills more quickly, he'd feel less guilt, but he won't buy that. There's also the clothes problem, not to mention his obsession with the number six. On the positive side, I have seen a lot of improvement in his choice of socks. This gives me hope for the future.

Herald: One last question. If someone were to meet Sherman, what advice would you have for them?

Dr. Frodsky: If anyone reading this runs into him, please remind him that he owes me money. And whatever you do, don't make fun of his shoes.

[2/1/90]

Brotherly Love

My brother recently published an article about brothers for a national magazine. Naturally, I was envious. I have to admit that the article was good, but I don't think it said enough about the intense sibling rivalry that brothers typically have.

We men can go on and on about how much we love our brothers, but the truth is that everything is fine as long as we are doing better than they are.

It all started with Cain and Abel, of course. As you might recall, Cain was a farmer and his younger brother, Abel, was a shepherd. Both of them tried to impress God, Cain with his produce and Abel with his sheep. God was more impressed with the sheep, and this made Cain pretty upset. To make a long story short, Cain slew Abel and eventually moved to the land of Nod.

Actually, there was more going on than God's preferences. Whenever Eve served dinner, she always gave Abel a slightly bigger portion, causing Cain to scream out, "He got more than me!" Not only that, Abel was a better soccer player than Cain and got higher SAT scores.

Typically, even when one brother appears to be very helpful to the other, he is actually trying to undermine him. Take the case of Vincent van Gogh and his younger brother, Theo. A recent *New York Times* book review discussed a biography of Vincent, which describes the well-known and very sad story of an artist who could not sell any of his paintings in his lifetime, paintings which are probably now worth a total of a billion dollars or more.

According to the review, "Theo had tried for years to sell them, not least in the hope of recouping a fraction of the money he had shelled out to support his hapless brother."

My guess is that Theo was insanely jealous of his brother's artistic abilities. He told Vincent that he was trying hard to sell his paintings, but in reality what he probably said to prospective buyers was something like this: "Look at this painting my brother Vince did. Do you believe this? He thinks he can paint, but I've seen 3-year-olds do better. And you won't believe what he's asking for it."

When something is a problem for us, we have sayings to try to make it look the opposite. For example, we keep saying over and over again, "You can't judge a book by its cover" to fight the powerful tendency we have to do just that, to judge people on how they look.

The expression (which became a hit song), "He ain't heavy, he's my brother," is another such saying. A more realistic statement would be, "Have you seen my brother? He weighs a ton!"

Younger brothers are a particular problem. Once

again, it all started with Cain and Abel. There was Cain, the apple (if you'll pardon the expression) of his mother's eye, until Abel came along. And so it is today.

There you are, the little prince, getting all the attention and, more important, all the toys, when suddenly, out of nowhere, here comes this upstart, about whom everyone oohs and ahs as they totally forget about you. And then, as the little brother gets a little older, your parents make you do something unthinkable. They make you *share*.

That's all bad enough, but younger brothers have a nasty way of being taller than you and often extremely good-looking. So you may have the utterly joyful experience at the age of, say, 14 or 15, of hearing a girl your age say of your 12-year-old brother, "Ooh, your brother is so cute!"

This is why I think the age difference between siblings is so important. If brothers are spaced about 15 to 20 years apart, sibling rivalry is not such a problem. It's much easier to handle comments about how cute your 12-year-old brother is when you are a successful lawyer, earning a hundred thousand dollars a year, and not a pimply-faced 5-foot adolescent.

The Bible doesn't say anything about heights, but something tells me Abel was taller.

Another problem is fame. It isn't easy to have a famous brother, especially if you're not doing anything very spectacular yourself. I mean, it's one thing to be

William James's brother Henry. William was a famous philosopher-psychologist; but Henry was no slouch as a novelist. I'm sure the rivalry was intense, but they each had their devoted audiences.

But what about Billy Carter, the late brother of the former president? He became a laughingstock, well-known only for his gas station, his beer-drinking and ultimately some kind of connection with Libyan strongman, Muammar Qaddafi.

I think he went to Qaddafi only because he was looking for someone who hated his brother as much as he did.

What it finally boils down to is parents. If parents find it inconvenient to space their children at 15- to 20-year intervals, they must bend over backwards to treat their kids the same, to not show favoritism

The whole problem with Cain and Abel probably started when Cain came to his mom and said, "Look, Mom, look at these beautiful vegetables I grew," and Eve said, "Big deal. Vegetables just sit there. Anyone can grow vegetables. If you won't go to medical school like your dad wants, you could at least do something challenging, like keeping sheep under control."

It was probably at this point that Abel walked in, and his mom said, "Oh, look at you, you've been working so hard, Abel dearest. Go in, take a shower, get the wool off. And then I'll make you a nice bowl of soup."

[10/11/90]

23

Games Couples Play

There are many words one can use to describe the phenomenon of marriage, but probably the most accurate word is "fun."

Yes, marriage is fun. And what keeps it fun are the games couples play. Some games can only be played when you are older and, preferably, when you have been married for a while. Other games are open to any couple.

In the former category is one my wife and I play more and more often. It's called the memory game. It's a simple game. All you do is try to remember something, like a name that, just a few years ago, you would have had no trouble remembering.

We played it the other day. We were in a restaurant and saw a girl in my son's high school class whom we had seen several times in plays. Surely, we knew her name. Of course, it was, it was...what was it?

"I think there's a B in the name," said my wife (I've changed the letter to protect the young woman's anonymity).

And we sat there, going over and over various possibilities. The girl and a friend got up to leave, but I had to know her name. I rushed over, introduced myself, and asked. She gave me that look so familiar to parents of teenagers, that look which says, "You're losing it, aren't you?" but told me her name. And we did have a partial victory. Her last name did start with a B.

I say "we" had a partial victory because, unlike many games, the memory game is a cooperative one. You try to see if, between the two of you, you can remember as well as one 21-year-old. (You should keep in mind that this game is only of interest to the two of you. No one else cares about the names you're trying to remember, or what city you bought that mug in fifteen years ago).

Another fun game is "Mine is (was) worse." This is a game in which each of you tries to prove that your father or mother is (or was, if deceased) worse than your spouse's. Of course, in the case of my wife and me, we play a less common variation, "Mine is better" (hope you're enjoying this, Mom!); but I know that other couples do have some trouble with their parents and play the "Mine is worse" game a lot.

It really is a terrific game. And, interestingly, though you and your spouse may not be able to remember the name of your child's teacher, you will be able to remember every rotten thing your parents did to you from the age of three on.

The "Mine are worse" game can be played by couples who have been married for a day or married for twenty years, but a game that is really only suitable for couples married a long time is "You ruined my life." As the years go by, it becomes harder and harder to blame our parents for the mess we have made of our lives. And no one in his or her right mind is going to blame themselves. So who is left but your spouse?

This is really a great game, which can be played any time and has numerous variants. No one ever really wins the game, but you can score minor victories with surprise attacks. If you're in the middle of a big fight, telling your wife she's responsible for every disappointment in your career history will be something she'll expect. So to do well at this game, wait for moments like this:

You've had a really nice Sunday together, have gotten along well, and have just returned home from a good dinner at a restaurant.

She: That was great, honey. I love you. You're the best.

He: Easy for you to say. I have to go to that same miserable job tomorrow. It's all your fault. If you had been willing to let me just try out – just for a year or two – that idea I had to start my own pet store, we could be rich by now.

She: But you're scared of animals, remember?

He: Yeah, but that was the selling point. "I got over my fears; you can too." I could've done it. I coulda been somebody. I coulda been a contender.

Some games are played throughout marriage, but how we play them changes. Some years ago, when her husband was alive, comedian Joan Rivers described a game married people play called "Catch me, catch me."

"They run around the house, with the pursued partner yelling 'Catch me, catch me!'," Ms. Rivers said. "We still play the game," she added, "but now we walk."

Finally, there is a game which isn't really a game, but more a recognition of the reality of getting older, having more obligations, kids in the house, etc. It gets its name from the punch line of a wonderful joke I heard from my wife's late great-uncle. The joke involved three elderly men lying on a beach and what they say when a young woman walks by in a skimpy bathing suit. It's called "Wasn't there something else we used to do?"

If you don't get it, you're still relative newlyweds. Enjoy!

[3/28/91]

27

Dysfunctional Families

The buzz term of the 1990s is "dysfunctional families." So many people seem to come from dysfunctional families that it's hard to believe there are any *functional* families. And if someone does come from an okay family, they certainly don't want to admit it. Not only will everyone else be envious of them, but they will lose the major excuse all the rest of us have for why we're so messed up.

There are so many different types of dysfunctional families that it would take not just a book, but many books to describe them all. But I'd like to describe four basic types, and I'll do so by little snippets of conversation.

First, there is the family in which the major problem is *breakdown in communication.* The scene is the dinner table. Everyone who comes from a dysfunctional family knows that it's at the dinner table where all the pathologies emerge in one way or another.

Father: I can't believe the day I had at work today! I thought I was going to go out of my mind. I can't stand that place anymore. I've gotta get out.

Son (age 14): Hey, Ma, you know I can't stand this kind of soup.

Daughter (age 9): Ma, my soup is too hot.

Mother: Don't complain to me, complain to your father. He likes this kind of soup.

Father: If I didn't need the money, I'd quit in a minute.

Daughter: I got a 100 on a spelling test today.

Son: Dad, whaddya think of Nolan Ryan? Seven no-hitters! And he's a year older than you!

Mother: The tax bill came today.

Father: I've been there more than 15 years. It's like I never existed.

Less common, but more common than we'd like to believe, is the *caninecentric family*, where everything revolves around the dog. This type of family is generally found in urban and suburban environments, where dogs have to be kept inside much of the time, walked on leashes, etc. The dog is like a perpetual child. In rural areas, where dogs are often free to roam, they are like teenagers, who may ultimately leave altogether.

The following shows a typical interaction in a caninecentric household. It's morning, and the family is about to have breakfast.

Mother: Robert, did you take Angel out for her walk?

Robert (age 12): No, I thought it was Mike's turn.

Father: No? You said no? No wonder she's all upset. Look at her. How would you feel if you had to go to the bathroom and no one would let you?

Angel (age 2): Woof, woof.

Robert: It's Mike's turn, it's Mike's turn!

Mother: Turns? You talk about turns? Look at her. She's so beautiful. And you talk about turns!

Mike (age 10): It's not my turn. I took her out yesterday morning.

Angel: Woof, woof, woof.

Father: Oh, Angel, my little Angel, I'll take you. No one else cares about you the way I do, precious one.

Mother: No, Bob, I'll take her. She loves me to take her. Everyone knows I'm her favorite.

Robert: Mom, Dad, I forgot to tell you. I got in some trouble at school yesterday.

Father: You, her favorite? Are you kidding? Angel, baby, come here, come to papa...Angel, what are you doing? Angel! Oh no, now look at what happened. She's so embarrassed, but she had no choice. She'll never get over this.

Robert: I'm in big trouble at school. I may be suspended.

Father: Suspended? Big deal. You'll get over it. She won't get over this. Angel, come here, we're sorry. Oh, baby.

Perhaps the most common type of dysfunctional family is the family ruled by *guilt*. The key sign that this is the case is the frequent use of apologies in order somehow to ward off the guilt feelings. This does not work and leads to further apologies. Food is also frequently used to assuage hurt feelings.

It's Friday evening at about 8:30 p.m.

Father: Listen, everyone, I gotta get something off my chest.

Son (age 15): What is it, Dad?

Father: Shut up, shut up and listen. Oh, I'm sorry. I'm sorry I said that. Oh, God, why did I say that? I'm sorry.

Mother: You should be sorry, Frank. Why are you so edgy?

Son: Stay out of it, Mom. It's between me and Dad.

Mother (starting to whimper): Oh, I'm sorry, I'm sorry. Why do I always intrude? Please, both of you, forgive me.

Son: Forgive you? It's all my fault. I'm sorry, Mom.

Father: Your fault? I started all this. I'm the one who should be making the apologies. It's work that's getting to me, that's the problem.

Mother: Oh, Frank, how could I be so heartless? Please, let me make you something. I'll fix you a salad.

Father: No, let me make something for everyone. I've been impossible lately. In fact, let's all go out for some of that non-fat yogurt.

Son: Non-fat yogurt? Dad, get real. That stuff is pathetic.

Mother: Rich, stop it. You know Dad has cholesterol problems. You want to kill him?

Son: Oh, Dad, I'm sorry. Non-fat yogurt is great; it's the best.

Father: Don't be sorry, Rich. You shouldn't have to suffer because of my problems.

Another very common pattern of dysfunction is the *family triangle*, where the child learns he or she can play one parent against the other.

It's Friday night and Steve, age 16, wants to go out with his friend Peter, who is 17 and has a car.

Steve: So how about it, Dad? He's a good driver, and we'll be back by one.

Dad: One? Back by one? When I was your age, my curfew was 9:30. Eleven. You'll be back by eleven.

Steve: But, Dad, I'm 16. And your parents were too strict.

Mom: He's right, Jim. Peter is okay. He's only gotten two tickets.

Steve: Thanks, Mom, you're the best. And by the way, Mom, you look really terrific tonight. You really do.

32

Whaddya say, Dad?

Dad: I say nothing doing. Didn't Peter just get out of jail?

Mom: Jim, you're not being fair. You know Peter doesn't deal anymore, and look at Steve. He's a man now. And a very handsome one, I might add.

Dad: Well, look how he's doing in school. What was your average last report card?

Mom: Stop it, Jim. You know he tries. I saw him reading a book on Tuesday. I'll bet he studied at least an hour this week. Give the kid a break.

It's clear that what this family needs is a dog.

[5/9/91]

"Because I Said So!"

Psychology has long been fascinated by child development. Among those who have studied this are Freud, Piaget and Mr. Rogers. To summarize: Freud said kids were sexual from Day 1, and the only thing that changed was what they wanted to do and whom they wanted to do it with. Piaget said kids were not very bright and somehow got brighter as the years wore on. And Mr. Rogers says, "Kids, you're great, every single one of you, no matter how obnoxious people say you are."

Seen from this perspective, we parents are relatively helpless, the focus of our children's bizarre fantasies ("When I grow up, I'll marry Mommy!"), their lack of intelligence (a five-year-old really believes that if you pound a small piece of clay into a pancake shape, there's more clay) or their insistent protestations of innocence ("Daddy, Mommy's mad at me for no reason!")

Yet we are supposed to shape and control these sex-crazed, deceptively simple-minded young con artists. And we're not supposed to hit them, chain them to the wall or even call them names. Amazingly, most of us manage. We do so primarily with our words, which necessarily change as the years go by. How we try to control our three-year-old is very different from how we try to control our 25-year-old, but the things we say show a consistent pattern of change, a development, if you will.

So herewith are Sherman's stages of parent-child development , as typified by what we parents say to children at different ages in order to somehow exert our authority.

Stage 1. Nothing. (Ages 0-1). Nature, in her wondrousness, gives us a grace period of about a year, when we can control our children without the need for words. Sure, it's nice to talk to them once in a while, and to hug them at least once a week, but babies have the great advantage of being small, portable and helpless. You can easily carry a baby from one room to another.

Try doing this with an 18-year-old.

Stage 2. "No!" (Ages 1-2). A baby's second year is a delight. They typically learn to talk and to walk, and some of the most precocious may even let you start to toilet train them. Best of all, a loud, firm "No!" will generally stop a child this age in its tracks if he or she is, for example, about to hit the stereo with a hammer or eat a pencil.

Stage 3. The helpless hiatus (Age 2). The "terrible twos" are very real. At this age, children cannot be reasoned with or ruled. They are totally out of control and are a great a danger to themselves and others, not to mention every one of your most valuable possessions. There's nothing you can do or say that will make any difference. The solution: Put your two-year-old in a comfortable padded cell and make sure to give him or her enough food and water.

Stage 4. "That's dangerous!" (Ages 3-6). At this stage, children are old enough to understand the concept of danger. By this time they have probably stepped on at least one bug and have thus learned about the concept of sudden death. You can actually reason with a child in this age group ("No, Patti, when you hold a scissors, you don't keep it right underneath your nose, pointing upward. And you don't run with it. What will happen if you trip?").

At this age, kids seem very grateful for this kind of advice. As teenagers they will, just to spite you, run with the scissors actually inserted into their nose.

Stage 5. "Because you're a big boy/girl." (Ages 6-12). Starting at around age six, for some unexplained reason, children like to feel like they're growing up. You often can get them to stop doing something silly or dangerous by invoking the image of the "big boy" or "big girl." It is, however, important to get it right. If you tell your son Tom that he really should remember to flush the toilet because, after all, "You're a big girl now!" he will probably get quite upset.

Stage 6. "I'm still bigger than you." (Ages 12-14). By age 12, children are able to reason so well that previous arguments for or against various behaviors won't work any more. You will find yourself becoming childlike and saying things like "Because I said so, that's why," or the even more infantile "Because." In desperation, you may say (if it's still true), "I'm still bigger than you" or, if desperation becomes even more intense, simply "Yaaaaaaheeeee!"

Stage 7. "You're not 18 yet." (Ages 14-18). We now enter what can euphemistically be called the Impossible Years. The books on child development say, "Your child will now be asserting his or her independence," making it sound kind of exciting and inspiring, sort of like the American Revolution. Well, remember, blood was shed in the American Revolution, and George Washington was one tough cookie.

The teenager shows the remarkable ability to be utterly charming with everyone else but like Frankenstein's monster at home. He is probably bigger than you. She may offer perfect arguments why she should do something like going cross-country on a motorcycle. But you still have the law on your side. They're not 18 yet.

Stage 8. "I'm still your father/mother." (Ages 18 and up). Uh-oh, your child is now 18. He or she is legally an adult. But don't despair. You can now start using the tool that will aid you for the rest of your life: guilt.

Introduce it gradually. At first you can say, "I'm still your mother (or father)" with power. After years of conditioning, the 18- or 19-year-old still responds to this. By the time your child is 30 or so, you'll have to say it differently, that is, in a kind of plaintive, little voice.

Relax. Over the years, you can use a wide variety of statements to keep your adult child in line, like "After all I did for you..." "Don't you care about me?" and "You know, I'm not going to live forever." If you feel funny about using guilt directly, shift the focus to your spouse by saying something like "Sure, go ahead, do it. You know it will break your mother's heart."

Or, if you really want to continue the fun of dysfunctional family life, say, "Why can't you be more like your brother/sister?" Then, eventually, your 30-year-old will find himself sitting in front of Mr. Rogers, who's telling him he's wonderful.

[3/19/92]

38

Marital Counseling

For those who have never been married, or for those who are married but have never sought marital counseling, the term may seem a bit mysterious and possibly even forbidding. But the reality is that marital counseling is a very simple, matter-of-fact procedure that most couples would benefit from, even if they don't feel that their marriage is in serious trouble. Because, let's face it, your marriage is in trouble. The big question is, How you do you keep it from becoming big trouble?

To help readers appreciate what goes on in a typical counseling session, I prevailed upon a marital counselor to let me tape-record her sessions with clients. This violated a major ethical principle of therapy, since the clients were not informed they were being taped. But upon completion of the taping, I offered large sums of money to the clients to allow me to publish excerpts from their sessions. They argued about it, and this became the major theme of a future session -- which I did not tape.

The couple, who I'll call Bob and Laura, have been married for ten years. They are both professionals -- he's a lawyer, and she is an accountant -- and they have no children. The major issue that's causing them problems is Bob's obsession with sports. He plays whenever possible and watches when he doesn't play. Laura could care less. She has no particular obsession, but has what Bob sees as an overly close relationship with her mother.

What follows is a brief excerpt from their first session with a counselor, who is an MSW.

Counselor: Hi, guys, how's it goin'?

Bob: It's going fine. I don't know why we're here. She dragged me here. There's a big game on right now, and I'm gonna miss at least the first half, and for what?

Counselor: Laura, why did you want to come here?

Laura: Isn't it obvious? All he cares about is sports. My mother warned me about this. We had our wedding date all set, hundreds of people were invited, and then we had to change the date because of some game. A game, for God's sake! As my mother said to me just this morning, "So how is Mr. Sports doing these days?" She's right. That's all that counts in his life, sports!

Counselor: Bob?

Bob: Oh, I see, you're taking her side. Well, even if I'm alone on this one, I'll be the winning team. Sure, there are two outs in the ninth in this marriage, but I'm going to hit a home run. Maybe I can't get a touchdown, but I'm definitely in field goal range. How can she say sports is all I care about? It's her mother that's put her up to this. She's much too involved with her mother. And her mother is a Mariners fan! A Mariners fan, do you believe that?

Counselor: Laura?

What is most important to note in the above is the subtle way in which the counselor helps steer the session. A little later in the session we can see the progress that is being made.

Counselor: Bob?

Bob: And there were only 35 seconds left in the game, and she says, "It's my mother on the phone, Bob, and she wants some legal advice." Legal advice? The Knicks were three points down, with 35 seconds left. What could be more important than that?

Counselor: Laura?

Laura: More important? My mother had a major legal question. She had tripped in her driveway and wondered if she could sue herself. I'm never too busy to help Bob's mother when she has a question about taxes. Basketball isn't more important to me than helping *his* mom.

Counselor: Bob?

But to see the real progress in marital counseling, we have to jump ahead to a later session. The following excerpt is from the fifth one.

Counselor: Bob?

Bob: I'm doing better now. I didn't watch any sports for three hours last night. It was hard, but I did it. By the way, do you know what happened in the Yankee game?

Counselor: Laura?

Laura: He says he's doing better, but I don't know. I know I'm improving. I went a whole day without talking to my mother last week. But then, when I did talk with her, she said, "So how's the human stadium doing? Does he talk to you between innings, at least?" But he does talk to me between innings. At least up until the 6th or 7th.

Counselor: Bob?

Bob: Sure, she went a whole day without talking *to* her mother, but all she did was talk *about* her mother. And her mother is way down in the standings as far as I'm concerned. She's got a team batting average of about .150, and an ERA of about 16. Every time she opens her mouth, that woman hits into a triple play.

Counselor: Laura?

However, the true success of marital counseling can be shown in a still later session. Let's listen in to a little bit of Session 10:

Counselor: Bob?
Bob:
Counselor: Laura?
Laura:
Counselor: Bob?
Bob:

Bob and Laura have now reached the kind of marital nirvana few couples attain. They now communicate silently. There is no need for words. Words can hurt, especially when men and women continue to speak their mutually unintelligible languages.

I'd like to go on with all this, but we've got to leave soon to visit my wife's parents. The real problem will be what time we leave tomorrow so as not to miss any of those NFL playoff games.

[1/21/93]

42

Free Association

A common technique in psychotherapy is free association. The patient lies down and says whatever comes to mind. The therapist, if he or she can remain awake, occasionally says "mmmhmmm" or, when feeling particularly insightful, says something more profound, like "yes" or "say more about that."

Somehow, miraculously, this leads to incredible insights by the patient. Not that these insights help him feel better or have a more productive life. But there is something very exciting in finally understanding why you feel so troubled all the time. I mean here it is, all these years you thought it was your cat who was making you unhappy, and now you realize it was your mother. How freeing! Not for you, of course. Your mother died five years ago, so you can't re-establish a good relationship with her. But you and your cat will be able to have a new bond that will be obvious to everyone.

As an experiment, I have decided to do this column by free association. I know there are some wonderful creative ideas sitting in my head, blocked by my own self-censoring. So I am going to lie down and write down whatever comes to mind. I will be both patient and therapist.

Me: Wow, Dr. Mark, it sure is hard to write while I lie down.

Dr. Mark: Mmm-hmmm.

Me: You know, Dr. Mark, sometimes I get really angry that I'm paying you so much money, and all you do is go "Mmm-hmmm." Could you say something different once in a while, please?

Dr. Mark: Yes. Go on.

Me: Thank you. I just had an insight! I'm never satisfied with people's responses to what I say. No matter how they respond, it's never right. I'm so ashamed. You say "Mmm-hmmm" and I object. If you said "Aha," I'd object to that too. Dr. Mark, you're brilliant.

Dr. Mark: I think we're making real progress this morning. Please go on.

Me: It doesn't matter what people say. People are just people. They are doing the best they can. Why do I always expect them to be different? I'll bet some people aren't even happy with all the things I say. I mean I think what I say is fine. But maybe they don't. But that's their problem. I'm okay, Dr. Mark, I'm okay. Aren't I, Dr. Mark, aren't I okay?

Dr. Mark:

Me: Dr. Mark, Dr. Mark, say something. Tell me I'm okay.

Dr. Mark:

Me: Dr. Mark, are you all right? Why don't you talk? Say something. Wait. I know. You want me to go on. Why do I have to ask you if I'm okay? I *am* okay. I don't have to ask anybody. What do they know anyway? Who cares if everyone else thinks I'm an idiot? They're idiots anyway. That's it, Dr. Mark, I just realized the answer. It's the answer to everything. We're all idiots. Every one of us...But not you, of course. Not you, Dr. Mark. You're smart. You're not an idiot.

Dr. Mark: Yes. Please go on.

Me: Maybe we're not all idiots. Maybe we're all geniuses. I like that idea better. Of course, if we're all geniuses, you're a bigger genius than most of us...

Dr. Mark: Mmm-hmmmm.

Me: I mean "than *any* of us." You're a bigger genius than any of us. You're the biggest genius. Your geniusness is so overwhelming that I can barely speak when I think of it.

Dr. Mark: Good. Please say more. Whatever comes to mind.

Me: I just thought about our family dog. I don't know why. I haven't thought about him in years. His name was Ruffruff. Did I ever tell you that, Dr. Mark? Did I ever tell you about Ruffruff?

Dr. Mark: Go on.

Me: Do you know why we called him that? My father thought of the name. When our dog barked it sounded just like "Ruff, ruff," so my dad said, "Let's call him Ruffruff." Me and my brother and sister all got very excited about this. We thought it was a great name. But my mother wasn't that excited, as I recall. I think she said something a little critical.

Dr. Mark: Yes. Go on.

Me: I think she said, "That is the dumbest name I have ever heard, and I've had enough. I'm leaving you." And she left. She packed up and left. I've always blamed the dog for this, but I realize now that there must have been more going on.

Dr. Mark: Mmm-hmmm.

45

Me: Well, when Mom left, us kids wanted to get rid of the dog. I think we were ready to kill him, or at least bring him back to the pet shop, but Dad said no. He said, "We'll keep Ruffruff. It's going to be a little rough around here with Mom gone, so the name Ruffruff will remind us of that. Get it, kids, get it? Rough, rough." And then Dad became hysterical, as he often did over his own puns. I think Dad lost it a little at that point. When people would call and say, "How are you doing?," he'd sort of bark. He'd say, "It's rough, rough." And he did become very attached to the dog. I think it was a little extreme.

Dr. Mark: Yes.

Me: You know Dad was a lawyer, and one time he sued the New York Yankees because they wouldn't let Ruffruff into the Stadium. Ruffruff actually had his picture in the New York *Times*. In fact, Mom called that day. We hadn't heard from her in a while, but she called. She was still not too happy. Dad said, "Didn't he look great in the picture?" I'm not sure what Mom said, but it couldn't have been too nice, because then Dad said, "Well, he's not a puppy any more, so what do you expect?"

Dr. Mark: I'm afraid our time is up for today.

Me: Ruffruff. Ruffruff. It wasn't you. You were just the catalyst.

Dr. Mark: That's it for today.

Me: Ruffruff. Ruffruff.

[7/21/94]

The Feminist Test

"Am I a feminist?" Today, as never before, millions of women are trying to answer that question. It's a much harder one to answer now than it was, say, twenty years ago. Back then, for most women (and men) feminism simply meant believing in equal opportunity for women and equal pay for equal work. Could anyone justifiably argue against that?

Today, with issues like politically correct language, office ogling, distribution of housework, and the position of toilet seats, the definition of feminism is not so clear. And many women are confused (in contrast to men, *all* of whom are totally lost).

To help reduce the confusion, what follows is a sample of items from the recently developed Feminist Inventory of Selected Topics (FIST). Try taking this little test--designed for women--to see whether or not you are truly a feminist. Don't expect any kind of scale at the end to tell you what your answers mean. Since I am a member of the patriarchy, any scales that I give will immediately be suspect. But I'll have to be honest and tell you that for each item, I do believe there is one clear-cut feminist answer.

1. Which of the following best describes your feelings about men?

    a. The majority of men are no good.

b. Ninety-nine percent of men are no good.

c. All men are no good.

2. You have just come home after a hard day's work. Your husband has just vacuumed the house for the very first time, and as you walk in the door he announces this. "Hi, honey," he says. "I just vacuumed the whole house!" Your response?

    a. Thanks, honey, that's wonderful. I really appreciate it.

    b. Yeah, good.

    c. Big deal. I do it all the time. What do you want, a medal?

3. You are planning your son's 8th birthday party, and he tells you the names of the kids he wants to invite. You notice that none are girls. What do you say to him?

    a. Gee, Tiger, what about Wendy? Isn't she your friend?

    b. Okay, sweetie, but if you don't want them to see your dolls, you're going to have to put them away yourself.

    c. Your choice, Buster. Either half the kids you invite are girls or there's no TV for a month.

4. The appropriate age to begin calling a human female a woman (rather than girl) is:

    a. 18

    b. 16

    c. 2

5. Heterosexuality is:

a. One heck of a lot of fun.

b. One alternative among many for human sexual expression.

c. A patriarchal plot to continue the behavioral and intellectual subservience of women.

6. Men's attraction to young, beautiful women is:
a. A natural consequence of evolution.
b. Due to a combination of biology and learning.
c. Strictly due to television ads. If it weren't for television, men would not even notice young, beautiful women.

7. A man complains to you that he feels he has been denied a job because preference was given to a female applicant. Your response?
a. Well, I feel for you. Affirmative action is still necessary to correct inequities. But keep trying. You'll find something.
b. Are you sure it was that? Maybe she was just better than you.
c. Nyaah-nyaah-nyaah-nyaah-nyaah.

8. You are single and 36 years old and have been going out with a man for two years. He proposes marriage. Your response?
a. Yes, yes, yes. Oh, yes.
b. Maybe. Have your lawyer talk to my lawyer about the contract.
c. Marriage is a patriarchal institution invented for the benefit of men. Its value for women is very limited. It is an ancient and outdated custom. However, for the moment, I'm willing to overlook all that, and, oh

Lord, yes, yes, I'll marry you.

9. You see a silly "feminist test" in a newspaper column. Your response?

a. Okay, it's important to have a sense of humor about things.

b. What's this guy's problem?

c. It's that stupid First Amendment again. If we could just repeal that, our country could be on its way to genuine freedom.

[4/27/95]

The Signals Of A Love In Peril

Lately, it seems, about one out of every two couples I know appears to be in the throes of major marital problems. Everyone knows that the divorce rate showed that incredible nearly vertical rise between 1965 and 1975, but it seemed that in the last 10 years or so things had improved a bit. So what's going on?

I'll be darned if I know. But I have noticed that there are some danger signals to watch out for. These are signs that your marriage may be headed for trouble or is already in trouble, and it is wise to be alert to them. This is not because this means you'll be able to save your marriage, but so you can get a good lawyer as quickly as possible.

1. *Your spouse suddenly becomes more loving than usual.* A basic principle of both physical and mental health is that any sudden change is worthy of attention and could signal problems.

In psychology, for example, a sign of possible emotional distress is a sudden and persistent change in sleeping habits.

But someone being more loving? How could that be bad?

Well, everyone knows that as marriage progresses through the years, passion fades. In fact -- let's be honest with each other -- it disappears. In a healthy marriage, both partners tacitly accept this, and neither one talks about it. But if one partner finds it hard to accept this law of married life, he or she may try to rekindle the spark by saying and doing those things he or she used to do, like saying "I love you" more than once a month.

Uh-oh. Someone has noticed the cooling of the libido. Now it's something you'll talk about. The sleeping dog has been kicked, and he's starting to growl.

But this is nothing compared to another possible reason your spouse may be whispering all those sweet nothings in your ear after having not done so for 20 years, and this is that he or she is attracted to someone else, or, God forbid, is having an affair. To throw you off track, your partner will shower you with kisses and words of endearment.

So what should you do if you're the recipient of a sudden increase in apparent affection? You will be sorely tempted to surrender to it. After all, who doesn't want to be kissed by their spouse and told that they're loved? But then you've given your partner the upper hand. So do yourself a favor. After that first surprisingly intense kiss or the even more surprising, "Oh, I've never loved you so much as I do this very moment," excuse yourself and call your lawyer.

2. *(For husbands only). Your wife announces that she is going back to school.* This announcement is typically a death sentence for your marriage. It's over. Faced with your wife being out of the house much more, and you having more household and childrearing responsibilities, you may protest. But if so, you will be seen as trying to stifle her growth. And besides, it

doesn't really matter what you say. If your wife wants to go back to school, she will go back to school.

And what will happen in school? Well, for one thing, since all the guys there haven't been married to your wife for 12 years, they will see her as she truly is, a very attractive woman. And professors will notice that she is also a very intelligent woman. And, worst of all, she'll take women's studies courses and discover the countless ways she has been oppressed by men, most especially you.

I can tell you, after all this, don't expect your wife to come home and happily do the dishes.

3. *Your spouse starts using words like "space" or "boundaries" a lot.* Back in the '60s, a sure sign your relationship or marriage was in trouble was when your partner said, "I need my own space." This didn't sound so bad at first, but it often turned out that this space was at least 2,000 miles away from your space.

One still hears that expression once in a while today, and it is still a danger signal, but the new early symptom of serious marital illness is the word "boundaries," as in "I've got to establish boundaries."

Husbands will hear this more often than wives, as the former often already have thick, impenetrable boundaries. The first time your wife says it, she will say it gently, and you will be tempted to get into a discussion of what it means and how you can change so as to make her happy. My advice: Go ahead, but only *after* you've spoken to your lawyer.

Space does not permit me to do more than simply mention several other early warning signals that your marriage may be in trouble. But, for better or worse, here they are:

- Your spouse mentions the name of another person of your gender more than three times in three days.

- Women: You see your husband talking to a younger woman.

- Men: You see your wife talking to a taller man.

- Your spouse says he or she is leaving you.

- Everything seems fine.

[7/20/95]

Real Men Don't Write Columns

Last June my wife gave me, as a Father's Day gift, a copy of Dave Barry's very funny *Complete Guide to Guys*. I did enjoy reading it, but his discussion of such topics as home repair reminded me of something I often find hard to face: By traditional standards, I am not a real man.

Well, technically, of course, I am. But that's just biology. I have come to conclude that I have about as much in common with some men as I do with this computer screen. It's like we're different species.

One of my kids has a friend whose father is what I think of as a real man. He's tall, works at a traditionally male occupation, essentially built his own home, knows a lot about cars and just exudes a confidence which I rarely feel except when telling someone how to get to my house from the New York Thruway. I enjoy talking to this guy (and my son always has a nice time at their house), but I always feel short and silly.

It's not that I'm incompetent or without value. It's just that if there were any kind of a crisis whatsoever, it is very clear that you would want him and not me. In fact, in today's gender-crazy world, isn't that what we mean when we think about what it means to be a "man"? Doesn't it imply someone who can come through, who can do what needs to be done?

I think this is what it means to be a woman too.

So where does that leave me?

I started reflecting on this the other day because suddenly, for no obvious reason, I started thinking about the word "drifter." You know how you read in the papers sometimes about a man who gets into some kind of trouble, and they describe him as a "drifter." Surely there's a type of real man. Have you ever heard of a woman described as a drifter?

Now drifters don't strike me as responsible types, like my son's friend's father. So that shows that you can be a real man at the opposite extreme. You do get the feeling, though, that as a drifter drifts, he often fathers children with whom he has no contact whatsoever. One might ask, How can a drifter father children? Why should a woman go to bed with a drifter?

Well, that's because drifters are probably pretty cool. They are manly. Imagine a woman walking into a bar. On one stool sits a college professor, someone who measures everything he says, someone for whom political correctness has become an obsession, someone who is an expert on Kant. On the other stool sits a drifter. Now she doesn't know he's a drifter (he might not know it either, since drifters often feel they are going to stay where they happen to have drifted), but what she does see is that he's big (it's very hard to drift effectively if you're small), and he's exuding that manly confidence. And he's noticed her and isn't hiding it. The professor has noticed her too, but he's worried that if he looks at her for more than two seconds he'll be accused of ogling.

So where is she going to sit? Does she want to hear about German philosophy from a "man" who's afraid to look at her, or does she want to know how it feels to be in a rodeo, how it feels to ride a bucking bronco? As a kid I got scared when I rode the carousel and the "horse" I was on went up and down. But there are men out there who get on bucking broncos, and I suspect that some of them, at least, are drifters.

Is there any way I can become a real man? The drifter route is out for me. I find it hard to be away from my family for more than six hours at a time, so the idea of drifting from city to city holds little appeal. So I guess the only way to go is the know-how-to-do-stuff path. Since my most recent adventure with household items was to break a light fixture which I accidentally bumped with one of my textbooks, I don't think this is going to work either.

But wait a minute. Maybe this can be the beginning. I'm not going to be intimidated by this broken lamp. This is a challenge. I can do it. Yes, I know what to do. I'll call my son's friend's father.

[12/7/95]

Not A Clue

My wife just told me about a news story she heard on the radio today. It seems that a young woman of 17 wound up in a New York City hospital, having some kind of nervous breakdown. She was somewhat amnesic, and all she knew was that she was from Florida.

Her father (divorced from her mom) somehow found out about this, and came up to get her. Had anything happened recently that might have driven her over the edge, concerned authorities asked?

"Not at all," said her dad. "Everything was perfectly fine. Well, okay, maybe there was one thing that might have upset her just a little. I just married her 18-year-old best friend. But she said she was fine with that. It wasn't a problem."

No problem? Is he kidding? When your son or daughter is 17, just looking at them the wrong way can lead to a lifetime of drug abuse; this guy goes and marries his daughter's best friend and can't imagine how this could possibly lead his daughter to take off for New York and forget her own name.

What's with parents of teenagers? Weren't they ever young themselves? Don't they (I should say "we" because my youngest child is 15) remember what it's like? I don't know. I guess that because young people are typically strong and healthy, and, as we love to point out, "have (their) whole lives ahead of them," it's hard for us, as parents, to imagine how and why they should be so troubled so much of the time.

Take pimples. Your teenager gets a pimple on his nose and he doesn't want to go to school. To you, this is absurd. "It's just a little pimple," you say. "No one cares about it."

Are you so sure? When was the last time you got on the bus to go to a huge prison-like building (aka high school), spent hours in rooms with 20 or more other people almost the exact same age as you, and then ate a barely edible lunch in a giant noisy room with hundreds of your peers, almost every one of whom had a blemish-free face and were attracting beautiful people of both sexes, while you sat there, with your only friend the absolutely nerdiest kid in the school, all because of this gigantic pimple, which your parents told you not to squeeze because, if you did, you could die from an infection that would go to your brain?

Teenagers are subject to daily humiliations of all kinds. For example, think about this. There you are, 17 years old, trying to get a sense of your own identity and realizing that, no matter what this identity is, surely it's something very different from your parents and who they are. "I don't know what I want to be," thinks the teenager, "but I know I don't want to be like them."

So you do everything you can to be different from your parents. You listen to music they couldn't possibly like. You get an earring, and if they get an earring, you pierce some other body part and wear a ring through it. They want you to apply to college, so you apply to art school.

And then, just when you are beginning to think that maybe you have finally started becoming your own person, a well-meaning relative says, "Jennifer, darling, I can't believe how much you're starting to look like your mother! And you sound like her too."

Obviously, the ring through your front tooth and the staple in your forehead wasn't enough. Now you're going to have to do something about your voice too.

...I just caught a little bit of that story on the evening news; yup, that guy really didn't think his marrying his daughter's friend was a problem for his kid. And would you believe, a Florida TV station is paying for them all to come back to Florida in style, for rights to the story? You know that some Sunday night down the road you'll be seeing this as a TV movie.

Doesn't it all make you yearn for the '50s, when most families were still together, sitting happily in front of their black-and-white TV sets watching shows like "Rin Tin Tin"? Okay, women were miserable and African-Americans were miserable, but for the rest of us, life was pretty grand, wasn't it?

But who's kidding whom? Even if you were one of the privileged people, life wasn't so easy, and if you were a teenager, life often felt like it was just too much to deal with. Now I realize that I should have been grateful that my mother didn't divorce my dad and marry my best friend. Actually, she didn't even like most of my friends. Thank God. I could have wound up a thousand miles from home, not knowing my own name.

[2/15/96]

60

Cool Guys

As regular readers know, one of my obsessions is what it means to be a "real man." Actually, it's broader than that. I'm obsessed with gender, in general. And one thing that particularly intrigues me is what attracts men and women to each other. Most specifically, what turns women on?

I know what turns men on. I know it's not politically correct to say this, but what turns men on is, oh, you know, do I even have to say it? If I say it, I'll get nasty letters, and I even could wind up on someone's "Wall of Shame." But I'm going to say it, because that's the kind of guy I am.

What attracts men? A nice personality, that's what. From the time I was a teenager, I can remember how groups of us guys would stand (then we stood; today we sit) around talking about girls' (women's) personalities.

"What do you think about Susan?" one of us would say. "Does she have a great personality or what? I just love the way she says hello."

"Yeah," another would add. "But what about Gail? Did you hear how nice she was to her friend Carol, when she broke her arm? When it comes to personality, that Gail is a '10'."

Okay, so what men are looking for is no mystery to me. But what are women looking for? All I know is

61

that in high school and through most of college they weren't looking for me. Or my friends. I remember in both high school and college hanging around with a bunch of guys. In each case, it was one small group of guys, and we had this in common: We didn't have girlfriends. It's not that we didn't want girlfriends (not that there's anything wrong with that), but we just didn't have them.

There were other guys we'd see in school during the day, but never at night. I thought those guys must have been studying. I realize now that I was wrong. *We* were studying, and then getting together to talk longingly about the girls we wanted to be with. The other guys? They were with those girls!

We were so nice. Why didn't the girls want us? I didn't know it then, but I know it now. Girls don't want "nice." They want "cool." You could be cool in various ways. One way was to look good. If you were really good-looking, that was enough. I knew some exceptionally good-looking guys in high school and college, and everyone wanted them -- women, men, children, grandparents, and even small animals. Looking back, I realize that none of my closest friends was exceptionally good-looking. Hard as it is to believe, even I, in my younger years, was not the heartthrob that I am today, when I'm often referred to as the middle-aged woman's Brad Pitt.

Where were those great-looking guys? They were with the great-looking (or even not so great-looking) girls. Or with other great-looking guys (not that there's anything wrong with that).

But you didn't have to be extremely good-looking to be cool. You could simply be mean and nasty. Or at least aloof. Not caring about anything was probably the most attractive quality a young guy could have.

You could see it happen:

Carol: Oh, hi, Mark. How's it going? Wasn't that math test hard?

Mark: Wow, yeah, wow. But I think I did okay. I studied so much. Those quadratic equations are tough though. How'd you do?

Carol: See ya later, Mark.

vs.

Carol: Hi, Chuck. How'd you do in that math test?

Chuck: Math test? What math test? Who cares about math?

Carol: Oh, Chuck, oh, oh, Chuck.

However, at the top of the heap, the guys whom the girls really wanted the most, were the bikers. At first, I thought this meant I had a great chance, since I owned this really nice Schwinn. So it came as quite a revelation to discover that the "bikes" in this case weren't bicycles but motorcycles. It had been hard enough persuading my parents to get me a bicycle; it seemed clear that a motorcycle was out of the question.

I started noticing them, the bikers. They wore leather vests. They had tattoos. They smoked cigarettes. What more could a girl want? And wasn't this every mother's dream for her daughter?

I did have my bike though. "Hi, Carol," I said one day. "Wanna go riding in the park with me this Saturday? We can ride our bikes down to the pond, and we can study. How about it?"

Carol was about to say her usual no, as sweetly

as she could, when along came Chuck. "Hey, beautiful," he said (I knew he wasn't talking to me). "How 'bout hoppin' on my Harley. Let's see if this thing can hit a hundred? Whattdya say? You wanna thrill?"

And she was off, off on the back of his real bike. And there I was, having an ice cream soda with my friends, wondering if I could ever be cool.

Ah, cool, shmool. How could speeding along on a Harley with a beautiful girl holding you tight ever compare with solving a really tough math problem?

[5/9/96]

You And Your Aging Parent

One of the pieces I wrote for this column back in its first year was called "Solving the Parent Problem." In that piece, I offered a simple solution for the difficulties so many of us experience when we try to maintain a good relationship with our aging parents.

I had noticed that no matter how difficult someone said her or his parent was, when I met the parent in question, she or he usually seemed very nice, intelligent and witty -- in a word, charming. So I suggested that to solve the parent problem, rather than visiting with our own parents, or having them visit us, we should do a parent exchange, so your parent or parents would visit me and mine would visit you. Under such circumstances, instead of spending our time with someone who we are pretty sure has ruined our life, and who is simply impossible to deal with, we'd be with a very interesting older person, who'd regale us with stories we had never heard before and around whom we would feel no guilt whatsoever.

Much to my surprise, my idea never caught on. So now I am forced to try to help my readers cope with what for many is one of the greatest challenges of their adult lives: how to have a harmonious relationship with their aging parents.

Let me be frank, however. There is no good

solution for this problem. In fact, it could be said that there is only one truly satisfactory way to deal with your aging parents:

Die young.

I hope my older readers won't take offense. After all, I am beginning to approach the status of the aging parent. How do I know this? Well, for one thing, I am repeating myself to my children. My 22-year-old son was recently up for a two-week visit with us, and, a day or two before he left, I mentioned the tape of a Seinfeld episode that I thought he might enjoy.

"Did you see the one where George and Jerry are mistaken for neo-Nazis?," I asked.

"Dad," he said, in a not too gentle manner. "Dad, do you realize that that's the third time in less than two weeks that you've mentioned that episode to me?" He seemed quite annoyed.

"I'm sorry," I said. "But that's what happens as a parent ages. My father used to say, `Have you heard this one before?' and then tell a joke he had told my brother and me at least twice. But we never said anything to him. I don't know if it was fear or politeness, but we just let him tell the joke. So why do you keep telling me so bluntly that I'm repeating myself?"

"Because I'm trying to improve you," he said.

Ah, youth!

As someone who is constantly analyzing every conversation I have, for whom life is like a movie that I feel I will have to review some day, I have begun to gather some information that might help all of us deal with our aging parents. This is no longer a problem for me, as my parents have died. Of course, I still have to deal with all the "baggage" and "old tapes," but at least that doesn't involve constantly worrying about whether I am seeing or calling them enough.

So in the brief space remaining, let me quickly discuss some of my observations.

First, the most problematic relationship appears to be daughter-and-mother. I cannot tell you how often I hear women say, "My mother is driving me crazy." As a matter of fact, my wife and I know of only two women who seem to have virtually perfect relationships with their mothers. We thought there was a third, but recently she called my wife and she too uttered that classic line.

The son-and-father relationship is different. For one thing, there aren't as many of these relationships, since fathers either abandon their children, or, if they stick around, they die. But many fathers do stay with their families, and have a powerful effect on their sons. However, rather than being driven crazy by their fathers, most sons are belittled and ridiculed by them, and therefore grow up saying, "My father destroyed me."

Asked about this, most fathers will say, "Oh, yeah? Is that what that little punk says? Well, I was just trying to make a man out of him. Just like my old man did with me."

You'll note that I haven't talked about sons-and-mothers or daughters-and-fathers. There's no need, since Freud and countless others, both before and after him, have gone into great detail on the bizarre aspects of these relationships. But let me mention just one thing for you to ponder: Why is it that I have heard women say happily, "I'm Daddy's little girl," but I've never heard a man say, happily or otherwise, "I'm Mommy's little boy"? I think that when we can understand and appreciate this difference, we will finally be able to bridge the gap between the genders.

The group that has really not received enough attention are the aging parents themselves. How do they see things? If a woman says, "My mother is driving me crazy?" what would her mother say about her daughter? How can you be the ideal aging parent? Should you simply send money? Should you say nothing at all about the obvious mess your son or daughter is making of his or her life? What do you do when your child introduces you to his or her significant other, and it becomes increasingly obvious that the love of your child's life is a right wing extremist?

Listen, I can't help you with this. If you haven't had your children repeat that Commandment, "Honor thy father and mother," at least ten times a day since they were little, any problems you have with them are your own fault.

[8/29/96]

Time For A Speak-Out

So now it's Bill Cosby. There, right in the middle of his grief over the horrible, the loss of his son, he confesses to what he calls a "rendezvous" many years ago. Not that he confessed out of the blue. He was confronted by charges of paternity by a young woman, and even as she was being arraigned on extortion charges, Cosby admitted that, yes, he had had an affair with her mother; as of this writing, he has said it's unlikely he is the father.

I'm not sure how women feel about Cosby's admission -- though I suspect it hasn't made him more popular with them -- but I think many men are relieved. In a sense, they feel vindicated. After all, this is Bill Cosby. Without a trace of irony, I really feel that Bill Cosby represents the best that America can do. He is a brilliant and extremely talented man, who has, from all appearances, been a wonderful parent while still working very hard and reaching huge levels of success in a public field. While obviously able to move comfortably in white America, he has shown pride in his African-American heritage. And he has been very charitable, giving large amounts of money to institutions and smaller amounts to individuals. He has always focused on the importance of education (a field in which he has a doctorate).

And now we find that even Bill Cosby, genuinely a paragon, has "fooled around." First it was Bill Clinton, who came close to having his presidential aspirations destroyed in 1992 when Gennifer Flowers came forward and said, "Hey, guess what?" But even those who like Clinton, and who unhesitatingly voted for him, don't see him as a moral standard-bearer (the Paula Jones thing is just the frosting on the cake). But Bill Cosby? Can no man be trusted? Who will be next?

Keep in mind that neither Clinton nor Cosby admitted their liaisons until the women involved came forward and accused them (actually, I don't remember Clinton ever formally admitting anything about Gennifer Flowers, but then again, he didn't inhale either). And that's got to send some fear and trembling into the hearts of the millions (worldwide, probably billions) of married men who have strayed. Guys can be pretty sure that if they even begin to achieve some kind of fame and fortune, a woman is going to come out of the woodwork and say, "Hello, remember me?"

Actually, it is typically the bright, talented, kind, funny, high-achieving men who are most at risk. If you marry a man because he is desirable, that means you are not the only woman who desires him. And sexual interest from women is very hard for most men to resist. When asked what kind of women he was attracted to, comedian Jimmy Walker said, "I'm attracted to any woman who's attracted to me." So to rephrase the words of an old popular song, "If you want to be happy for the rest of your life, be an uncharismatic man's wife."

Looked at in a certain way, this media frenzy over famous men's infidelities is just another escalation in the ever more bitter war between the sexes. They say that hell hath no fury like a woman spurned (or is it scorned?), and women all know that it is very embarrassing to a man to accuse him publicly of violating one of the Ten Commandments. Let's face it, no one likes to be caught violating a Commandment. It really does not look good on your résumé.

As for the "other woman," it's much harder to be angry at her. She is typically younger than the man, and while he may be a governor or an extremely successful entertainer, she is a virtual unknown, usually scraping by to make ends meet. So women know that in their attempt to bring the entire male population to its knees, this is a very strong weapon indeed.

Well, guys, it's time to take sides. Are we going to just let Bill Clinton and Bill Cosby swing in the breeze, relieved that everyone's paying attention to them so they won't notice us? Are we going to join the finger-pointing and feign incredulity at the indiscretions of our brothers? Or are we ready to do the unthinkable, and confess that we too have strayed?

Yes, that's right, I am suggesting a national speak-out, where men of all races and all strata of society will come together as one and say, "It's not just our president and one of our most beloved television personalities who have done this. We too have done it. We're not happy about it and we're not proud of it. But we have done it. It's who we are. Besides, none of us were as bad as John Kennedy, and he has an airport named after him!"

Who is ready to take this bold step? Which man will come forward, without being publicly provoked, and say, "I've had enough. I'm sick of living in fear. I confess."

Think of the relief, the oneness men will feel, when someone somewhere says, "I surrender. I'm not perfect. I'm not a saint. I'm just a flesh-and-blood man."

Then millions of other men can rally round this brave soul --and he'll need these millions of guys to protect him from his wife -- and finally, for once and for all, be able to drop their feeling of shame when they realize that they are not alone. For solidarity, even those -- it's gotta be several hundred thousand -- married American men who haven't once played around can say, "I've done it too."

Ultimately, this will also benefit women. They will realize there's nothing wrong with them. As usual, there's something wrong with us guys. Some day women as well as men will celebrate that great day when a man willingly stepped forward and said, "Yes, there was this time ten years ago..."

So who will it be?

It won't be me, of course, but who *will* it be?

[2/13/97]

Child's Play

As I get older, and deal with more and more responsibilities, I find myself looking back nostalgically at childhood. I tend to think mostly of the positive stuff and the fun stuff, which, of course, I didn't appreciate then. George Bernard Shaw said, "Youth is wasted on the young," and he had a good point. Incidentally, Shaw was only nine years old when he made that statement, showing that he was pretty serious as a child.

It is remarkable how different adult life is from the child's life, but the change from childhood to adulthood does not happen overnight, except in the case of the mayfly, which only lives for one day.

But for human beings, it's a slow process, and we don't even notice when the day comes that we no longer do the things children do -- such as somersaults.

Well, some people keep doing them, like gymnasts. But for most of us, the idea of doing a somersault seems a combination of silly and dangerous. I don't specifically remember my last somersault, but I do remember doing them. I remember that wonderful feeling as I gave my body that little extra push that propelled my legs over my head as I rolled over onto my back. I can't remember how my parents reacted to this, but since I was having fun, they probably disapproved.

Actually, I am sure they preferred having me do somersaults than the other activity I loved to do even more than somersaults, namely, spinning. "Don't do that," my mother would say. "You'll get nauseous." But I don't remember ever getting nauseous. What I do remember was that after you spun around for a while, and then stopped, the whole world seemed to spin. I loved this. I have to confess that I probably did it a little too often. Okay, today I can admit it: I had a spinning problem.

I quickly learned to spin in private. But my parents were very suspicious. There I would be, sitting on the floor giggling hopelessly as my room spun around, and I could hear my mother saying, "Are you spinning again? You know it's going to make you nauseous. You stop that spinning and come out here, right this minute!"

And if I didn't come out, my mother provided what is one of the negative things about childhood, something which you never hear adults say to each other, but which parents say to children all the time. You know, when the parent says, "I'm going to count to three, and if you haven't done such-and-such by the time I get to three, you're in big trouble."

Actually, my parents were very strict, and only counted to two.

"You come out here now," said my mom. "I'm gonna count to two and if you're not out here by the time I get to two, I'm not going to let you listen to the radio for a week."

And she'd start. "O-o-o-o-n-e," she said, dragging it out the way parents do, since they (well many of them, anyway) don't really want to punish their children, but just want to control them completely. I didn't budge. "One-and-a-half," she said, giving me yet another break. I still didn't move. I couldn't. I had overspun. I couldn't get up. "One-and-three-quarters," she went on. Uh-oh, I thought, I think she means it this time.

So somehow I got myself up and staggered out the door.

"I haven't been spinning," I said, as I grabbed onto my mother to keep from falling to the floor.

And talking about the floor, there's another difference between children and adults. Children, but not adults, spend lots of time playing on the floor. And why not? The floor is a great place to play. It's like a table top of unlimited size. The only problem is that sometimes your toys get stepped on or tripped over, and occasionally you get stepped on or tripped over. But everything in life has its dangers. Surely your parents preferred you playing on the floor than in the street.

One day, around 16 years ago, in the midst of a dry spell in my creative life, I decided to do some writing while sitting on the floor in order to see if this return to my childhood milieu might spark my creativity. So I brought my typewriter into the kitchen, put it on the floor, and began typing. And sure enough, I did have an idea, which ultimately became a magazine article.

I was quite excited by this, and asked my wife if it would be okay for me to do all my writing on the kitchen floor. She emitted a string of unprintable epithets in the middle of which I detected the word "no."

I was pretty upset by her response, but a few minutes of spinning was all I needed to calm myself down.

Lest you think my whole childlife was spent in solitary pursuits, such as somersaults, spinning, and playing alone on the floor, let me assure you that this was not the case. I would also be involved in something that, as an adult, I really miss.

I would be sitting there, tired of one more solitary game of Red Barber Baseball or one more spin of the little pointer of All-Star Baseball, feeling that even a somersault wouldn't get me out of my funk, when suddenly, miraculously, the phone would ring, and it would be one of my friends asking if I could come over to play. And so I was rescued.

We adults just don't do this, and maybe we should. Think about it. You're at home on a week-end. You've done some chores, you've looked at the newspaper, you're kind of bored.

The phone rings. It's your pal, Mike, and he says, "Can you come over and play?"

Reflexively, you think, "I'll have to ask my mother." But you don't have to. You're an adult now. Maybe somersaults and spinning might be too risky to your body and your furniture, but you can still play. And Mike's got one great floor.

[5/8/97]

Desperately Seeking Serenity

Over the last several years I have become more and more interested in living the good life, which I have come to realize doesn't mean the materially good life but rather the spiritual one. Obviously, I am not alone in this desire, since bookstores are simply filled with self-help books of all kinds, promising that if you follow this suggestion or that, your life will improve. And I believe this. So I buy a lot of those books, and not only that, I read them, and I try to follow their recommendations.

If anyone tells me how a particular book helped them, I go out and buy it. If an ad in the papers makes a particular book sound like it's THE answer to my problems, I buy it. If, in browsing around the bookstore, I notice a book that promises to change my life for better and forever, I buy it. At the rate I'm going, material success will be impossible, because of the financial drain of all this book buying. Thus, spiritual success will be all that is left to me.

But I have noticed a problem. I have become anxiously obsessed with achieving calm in my life. You see, not only do I buy lots of books, but if someone says something about how they solved this problem or that one, I not only listen carefully, but I write it down as soon as possible. I have come to realize that my life is more and more becoming a desperate search for serenity, which, in itself, is making me tense. I mean, I keep thinking, am I keeping up with the latest in self-help ideas? Am I doing enough?

I meditate, but I don't think I meditate for long enough each day. Yet, if I meditate longer, will I have time to do all the things I have to do?

And what about yoga? One of my favorite self-help books recommends yoga as a really good way to start the day. But I don't know how to do yoga, so I'll have to learn it. And that will be two more things I have to do -- the learning and then the doing. You know there aren't enough hours in the day to read spiritual literature, meditate, do yoga, and do the dishes. On top of which, once upon a time I thought I'd accomplish something big in my life. I thought I was going to write a best-selling book. But instead of writing a best-selling book, I read other people's best-selling books. And their books just tell me to relax, meditate, do yoga, and not worry about how little I get done. And while I'm relaxing and all that other stuff, they're writing another best-selling book and vacationing in Aruba.

One of my books says that I should "sit alone in quiet meditation at least twice a day for approximately thirty minutes in the morning and thirty minutes in the evening." Thirty minutes? At least twice a day? I feel rushed enough as it is, and I try to meditate for 20 minutes in the morning, period. While I'm meditating, other people are buying and selling stocks, writing, filing law briefs, filling people's teeth, and making business deals. And that's only 20 minutes. I'm already behind. If I make it half an hour, I'll fall even further behind. And then I'm supposed to do it for thirty minutes again in the evening? I don't get enough sleep as it is.

I'm telling you, this self-improvement business is utterly exhausting!

And it's not just the strictly spiritual side I work on. I also am well aware of how important proper nutrition and dietary supplements are. After all, I've read some Andrew Weil. Whether it's selenium, broccoli or tofu, I've got to have it.

But even that is not enough. I have to exercise. I have to run or use my exercise bike at least three times a week. Okay, okay, I know it should be four probably, but, listen, every once in a while I have to do some work, and I've got to allow time for "Seinfeld."

Do you realize that while I'm so busy trying to stave off despair and death, there are people who smoke 40 cigarettes a day? And not only that, they eat corned beef! And they've never heard of Andrew Weil. Maybe they don't feel great all the time, but they are doing something that I'm not doing: They're living!

I, on the other hand, have become addicted to self-improvement. Wait, I just had the idea for my best-seller: *Re-join the Rat Race: The Quickest Rats Get the Best Cheese.* As long as I'm rushing around anyway, why not make it for some noble purpose: acquiring huge sums of money? Did you ever notice that the only people who tell you that being rich isn't the answer to life's problems are the very rich authors of self-help books?

Listen to me. Obviously, I've strayed from the spiritual path. I guess it is time to add yoga to my ten-hour-a-day regimen of self-help activities. Or at least I'd better up my meditation time. And eliminate sugar from my diet. And coffee. Yes, and perhaps the time has finally come to cut out yeast.

[10/9/97]

Ready To Fly Solo

After all the revelations that keep coming out in newspapers and books these days, I don't think I have to be embarrassed to admit, right here in print, that I have been in therapy. Actually, several times. Okay, I'll be honest: I've been in therapy on and off since I was 21.

Right now I'm off. It was close to a year ago I said good-bye to my therapist.

His response was the usual.

"What do you mean by that?" he asked.

"I mean I'm done. You've helped me a lot, but now it's time to see if I can make it on my own. I'm ready to see if I can fly solo for a while."

"Just when did you begin to feel this way?" he asked, with that calm, infuriating manner he always had.

"To be honest," I said, "I've felt this way starting with the first session. The only reason I kept coming is for my parents."

"But your parents are dead," he said.

God, how can I leave?, I thought to myself. He's always saying these profound things.

I sat back down.

"Let's talk about your parents for a while," he said.

"No," I said. "We have been talking about my parents for five years. I'm talked out. Just how many times can I tell the story of why my father called me Pruneburger? My parents are gone. Can't they rest in peace?"

"I think you still have a lot of work to do," he said. "I don't think you're ready to go solo. You have a lot of unresolved issues."

"Well, you're right. So it's time for me to resolve one issue: How not to pay $100 a week just for the privilege of telling someone my deepest, darkest secrets. Was it worth the $500 it took for me to finally tell another human being that I still cry every night because Howdy Doody isn't on television any more?"

"It sounds to me like you still have a lot of anger," he said. "And you know, anger is..."

"Yes, I know, I know," I screamed. "Anger is simply a cover for fear. You're right, you're right. I am afraid. I'm afraid if I keep coming here I'm going to run out of money, and my dependence on you will never be broken. I'm a man. I have to be able to face life on my own. And I want to use the money for productive things, like gambling, alcohol, and contributing to the Bring Back Howdy Foundation...You make me furious. What does that mean? That I'm afraid of *you*? How could anyone be afraid of you? Look at you, sitting there so smug while this very minute real men are doing real men things like laying bricks, driving trucks, and searching for videotapes of the Howdy Doody Show."

"Let's talk about this 'man' thing for a while," he said. "Why is it so important for you to 'be a man'?"

"Oh no, not this again. The 'man' thing. Can't you see we're under attack? We've lost our identity. We've

81

become ashamed of who we are. Feminists have attacked us, and instead of fighting back we've simply lain down and said, 'Go ahead, step on me. Please. I know I've been bad.' It's like we're all a bunch of masochists. What would Buffalo Bob say about all this?...I hate to say this, but you're not a real man."

"Am too," he said.

"Are not," I said.

"Am too."

"Are not."

As had happened so frequently in recent weeks, our session had degenerated into a childish clash of wills. But he always had the upper hand because when all was said and done, I paid him, he didn't pay me. Yes, it was time to see if I could make it on my own.

I stood up.

"Jerry," I said. "I appreciate all you've done for me. Really. You've helped me to find myself. There I was, right under the coffee table. No wonder the dog kept barking at the coffee table. I came in here a sick man, but now I feel really healthy. I feel good about myself. I'm proud of who I am. I'm a man. I'm a husband and father. And, yes, I still miss Howdy Doody. I'm not ashamed to say it. There was something about that interaction between Howdy and Buffalo Bob that was beautiful. When Bob would say, 'Well, howdy, Mr. Doody,' all seemed right with the world. I'm still angry with Mr. Bluster, but I think I can forgive him today...Yes, I'm ready to see if I can do life on my own."

"I'll miss you," he said. And I could see that the tears were starting to come.

"Oh no, Jerry, not the crying again. I'm telling you, I'm outta here. Don't start with the crying. It won't work this time."

"You're such a great patient," he said, drying his eyes. "You've never called in the middle of the night because you couldn't remember the name of your first pet turtle; you never, not once, made threats on my life; you've got a good sense of humor; and, best of all, you're never late with your payments. Oh, I'll miss you so much. Do you really have to go?"

"Yes," I said. So I got up, put on my "Howdy Lives" cap, and left.

[10/23/97]

Wild Boys, Wimpy Men

There has been much written on what happens to girls when they reach the age of 10 or 11, that they somehow lose their self-esteem, and give up their own voice in favor of the prevailing male-oriented society. Magazines and bookstores are filled with the troubles girls have with body image, speaking up in class, and concern about their hair. *Reviving Ophelia*, about the travails of adolescent girls, has been a bestseller for several years.

I'm not saying this isn't a problem, but all this attention to the plight of girls has led our society not to notice what has happened to boys on their way to so-called manhood. Basically, what has happened is this: Men, who are constantly reading or hearing about how they should soften up, become more gentle and not be brutish, have changed. They have become wusses or wimps, or whatever term feels comfortable for you. However, this is not true of boys, who haven't yet read all this stuff by feminists, and who are still more dominated by their hormones and genes than they are by women, books, and the media. So what we see today, up until their adolescence, are males acting like males always have, except worse, and then, at age 17 or so, changing, wimping out, if you will.

Assertive, some say aggressive, behavior starts early for boys. Remember those stories last year about

6-year-old boys who got into trouble in school because they kissed girls in their classes? These boys hadn't read about self-restraint and sexual harassment yet, or perhaps they *had* read about President Clinton, and they just did what boys have always done (actually, in at least one of these well-publicized incidents, the girl seemed quite willing, but still the school was ready to suspend the boy).

By the time they are 15 or so, boys are not only still trying to kiss girls, but are also doing things which show even more nerve. Consider this story out of Lancaster, California, which appeared in the *New York Times* in November of last year. Under the headline, "Boy in Chimney is Freed by Firefighters," it read: "While defying his mother, a 15-year-old boy tried to get into his house by shimmying down a chimney but wound up stuck for 90 minutes before being pulled free by firefighters. The boy...got into an argument with his mother over when he should be home...The mother called the Sheriff's office after the boy started throwing objects around the house and causing other problems, witnesses reported.

"When deputies arrived, the boy climbed to the roof and refused to come down. At about 2:30 A.M., he tried to get into the house by climbing down the chimney...."

Yeah, I know, some psychologists are going to see this as an example of some kind of identification with Santa Claus, but not me. I see it as the last hurrah of wild masculine youth, a kind of "I'll show you, world!" Okay, okay, he got stuck. But it was a good try.

In contrast, consider a news story that appeared a couple of months earlier. While the main point of this story was why a second woman dropped out of the formerly all male Citadel ("...(a) College spokesman said...the woman...decided she did not want the military lifestyle"), the last paragraph said that "the college is looking into a complaint by a male student who left earlier this week. He said an upperclassman sprayed water into his face from a drink bottle...."

Oh, Lord, the horror of it! He got sprayed in the face with cold water! Surely, in any kind of warfare he would never face such brutal treatment.

Come on, give me a break. I assume this guy was about 18 at the time of the incident. And he had chosen The Citadel, so I assume he didn't see himself as a complete wimp. But something must have happened to him between 15 and 18. And if it happened to this guy, who had the nerve to try The Citadel in the first place, what's happening to other boys, who, intrepid as they may be, still shy away from that kind of rigor?

I am not suggesting that we encourage our sons to be aggressive or to engage in highly risky behavior. I don't approve of kissing unwilling girls or chimney-shimmying. I'm just saying it's time that America's boys keep a little bit of the masculinity they once had as men. Perhaps the best model would be someone in the middle ground, someone who can be a leader but still exercises caution, you know, someone who might try marijuana but wouldn't inhale.

[2/26/98]

86

My Son, The Rock Musician

It's 3:15 on a Sunday afternoon, and I'm feeling sleepy. This is not unusual for me on a Sunday, but today I have really earned it. My wife and I went to see our son's band play last night in New York City. They went on at a little after midnight and, even though we didn't stay for their second set, we didn't get home until 3:15 a.m.; I wasn't asleep until after 4.

This is what it means to be the supportive parent of a child in the music business. It means permanent hearing loss and the kind of late nights I tend to associate with people 30 to 35 years younger than me. This is not to say there isn't joy in it too. To see your son playing music with his best friend on a New York stage and remembering back to when they played in high school as part of a band called Urban Dirt is good compensation for coming home with your hair, your hands and all your clothes smelling of cigarette smoke.

Not that I'm envious, of course. How could any man envy a young guy who has very good-looking young women practically throwing themselves at him as he does something he loves?

But last night, as I stood in the back of this club in Greenwich Village and thought about trying to make my way to the front so my son would know I was there, I realized that no matter how proud we parents justifiably are of our children's achievements, not many of their jobs offer this possibility of actually watching them work.

Suppose, for example, my son were a physician. Do you think his patients would really appreciate it if, while he was performing a physical examination, I just kind of hung out and watched? I suppose if he were a lawyer, he might enjoy my coming into the courtroom as a spectator once in a while, but I do get immersed in things. It's one thing for me to sing along with his band's songs and clap and dance. Do you think my son would appreciate it if I suddenly yelled out, "Objection!," when the opposing attorney asked what I thought was a leading question?

I realize that in the hierarchy of occupations that, while it is prestigious, "rock musician" is not at the very highest level. What's up there are clearly "rocket scientist" and "brain surgeon," as in the expression, "You don't have to be a rocket scientist/brain surgeon to figure that out." For some reason we assume that rocket scientists and brain surgeons know more than the rest of us. I am sure that this is true about rocket science and brain surgery, but I know someone whose father is indeed a brain surgeon, and aside from his field of study, he doesn't seem to have a clue about the rest of life (just like me and everyone else I know).

Anyhow, if your child were a brain surgeon, do you really think he or she would like it if you stood there in the operating room, and periodically yelled out, "Good cut!" or "Watch that nerve!" And though I am not exactly sure what rocket scientists actually do, it seems that their work would not benefit from an interested parent standing nearby applauding as they did their rocket science.

And suppose your daughter were a psychotherapist? How do you think her patient would react if you sat next to your daughter as her patient discussed the details of the strange things that went on in her house when she was a little girl?

Let's say your son were a businessman, who had reached a high level in a major corporation. Do you think he'd want you there in the boardroom as he and his fellow board members discussed a leveraged buyout? If you're anything like me, you would probably be tempted to say, at a particularly crucial moment, "Excuse me, but what *is* a leveraged buyout?" which would probably lead to his corporate colleagues asking you to leave, followed by their firing your child.

And what if your daughter is a spy? Now that's a fine situation to be in as a parent, isn't it? It's bad enough you can't watch your child work (how does she explain what you're doing at top level meetings of the Politburu, whatever that is?), you really can't even tell people what she does. You have to make something up, like "She's in international trade," or "She's an exporter-importer." But that's not nearly as exciting as what she really does, and sooner or later you'll probably just blurt it out, possibly to someone who is in actuality spying for the other side, leading to her expulsion from wherever she is spying, and then World War III.

Okay, there are other fields where you can watch your child do his or her work. One of these is athletics. If your son or daughter is one of the one hundredth of one percent of the population who plays sports professionally, you can have the joy of watching him or her play for pay. But then, of course, since sports fans yell nasty things out all the time, you might have the upsetting experience of sitting next to someone who screams out at your son, as he gets up to the plate, "Ah, Murphy, you're through, you're washed up. You can't get a hit to save your life!"

So there's an advantage of being the father of a rock musician. Perhaps people in the crowd are saying nasty things about him, but I can't hear it. After a little while, I can't hear anything.

Of course, it could be worse. Suppose my son were a columnist. It sure would be a big whoop watching him type.

[3/26/98]

We're Perfect. And You?

Well, the holiday season is over; and with its end comes, happily, an end to those family letters that many people send with their cards. You know what I'm talking about -- those photocopied one- or two-page descriptions of just what has been happening to the Smiths or the Joneses for the past year.

What bothers me about these dispatches from the family front is how absolutely great everything is in other people's lives, how precocious their children are, what terrific trips the whole family has taken, and how, while the renovations to the kitchen were pretty disruptive for a while, now it looks just great and "we just can't imagine how we got along in the old one."

For example, here are some paraphrased -- and substantially revised -- excerpts from a holiday letter that a friend of ours recently received. I am changing names and other details to avoid being sued, but, given the nature of today's society, for all I know I'll be sued anyway. All I can say to that is this: I did not have sex with that woman, Monica Lewinsky!

So here are a few of those excerpts. The message starts off, "Greetings from the Smith Family. We wish you a healthy, happy holiday and New Year."

My feeling is, Why don't they just stop right there? Isn't that all you really want to hear from the Smiths, whom you haven't seen in 14 years anyhow and, to be honest, barely care about?

But, of course, like the beat, it does go on.

"John got a big promotion this year at Futurebright...As you have probably read in the papers, Futurebright is in the forefront of chemistry research worldwide...John is somehow surviving without baseball, but he is so busy with his hobbies and investments that it hardly seems to matter.

"Marcia is getting ready for graduate school...She will begin graduate studies next fall at the B.F. Skinner Institute for Advanced Study in Behavioral Methodology....

"David is now in the sixth grade, but is taking algebra at the high school. He is doing quite well, and the high schoolers love him...He is a terrific pitcher in Little League, and this year he took up golf!

"Endicott is now in kindergarten...He loves to read and write, and is making lots of friends."

I mean, look at that. Your family and mine have been having all kinds of problems, but for the Smiths things seem to be moving right along without a hitch.

Isn't it time for more realistic holiday messages? Wouldn't you get much less annoyed and disgusted if, instead of reading the above kind of family bragging, you got something that read like this?:

"The Jones family wishes you the best for the holidays. We've certainly had our ups and downs this year, and all I can say is thank God for Prozac!

"I'm happy to report that Bob's affair is finally over. All his jokes about 'If Bill Clinton can do it, why can't I?' were beginning to wear pretty thin. Unfortunately, just when he stopped seeing that other woman, he lost his job with Lotech. He was just one month away from full vesting for retirement, but we'll get by -- if Bob can finally hit it big with one of those hundred lottery tickets he buys every week.

"And Tim is finished with rehab! He's even talking about going back to school, although that might have to wait. It all depends on what happens when he goes to court next month.

"Jeannie had some troubles in college this year, mainly due to a bunch of very bad teachers. She told us that in all of her courses the exams were never exactly what she expected, and the grading was very unfair. She's on academic probation and is thinking of dropping out. She says she wants to find herself.

"We're excited about her new relationship. It's been three weeks now, so we're crossing our fingers that maybe this is the one. He's really very nice and says he is close to being divorced.

"And 'little Danny' isn't so little any more. He's the biggest child in his first grade class. His teacher says Danny likes to hit the other kids, but Bob's feeling is that the teacher is picking on him because he's so big. We recently had a knife incident, but I think it was blown way out of proportion. It was just a butter knife that Danny brought into school, and I think the suspension wasn't necessary.

"On a sad note, we had to put Puddles to sleep. They say you don't get attached to hamsters, but take my word for it, you do."

[1/14/99]

93

"I Do...Maybe"

My oldest son is getting married in June! He and his fiancée have been together for over five years, so I am hopeful and optimistic that they will have a happy and lasting marriage. But I do know that the statistics on marriages in our country are not terrific. Things have been a little better in recent years, but a substantial number of marriages still end in divorce. And among those that don't (or haven't yet), there are many marriages that you could hardly call "happy."

I've thought about this a lot. What amazes me is that, in spite of the obvious difficulty many, if not most, people have in staying married, the principles of marriage, as voiced in the so-called marriage vows, have stayed pretty much the same for hundreds (thousands?) of years.

Let's face it, if a car company made a car with the same failure rate as American marriages, either the federal government would step in and shut it down, or at least it would force the company to make changes in their manufacturing process. And yet we insist on holding on to our clearly obsolete wedding vows, and then wonder why so many of us can't stay together.

Well, someone has got to take the bull by the horns. So I'd humbly like to suggest a few, really minor, modifications to the vows, simply to make them easier to fulfill.

I think one of the hardest, at least for men, is

that one about "forsaking all others." You know, the pledge of fidelity. Lots of people have trouble with this one. President Clinton certainly did. His inability to stick with this vow virtually paralyzed Washington for over a year.

My suggestion, to avoid this kind of problem in the future, not only for presidential marriages but for those of ordinary people, is to make a slight change. Instead of "forsaking all others," why not make it "forsaking most others"? Or even "forsaking the vast majority of others." I think it's the "all" that causes the problems.

Then there's the "love, honor and cherish" part. This is already different from what it used to be for brides. Women used to be expected to say, "Love, honor and obey." But in the '60s, a lot of women said, "Obey? Yeah, right!" So soon both members of the couple were saying what the man had always been saying, that is, pledging to "cherish," as well as love and honor.

However, this certainly didn't slow the rate of divorce. The problem is that all that loving, honoring and cherishing seems so easy on your wedding day, when she is in her beautiful gown and he is in his tuxedo and everyone is sitting there crying. It's a whole different story when he's in his undershirt and she's in her sweatpants, and they've been together, bickering, for 25 years.

So why not be more realistic, and pledge what we really expect from each other years later: to be, well, tolerated.

Then there's the "for better or worse" portion of the vows. That's a tough one for many couples. The "better" part is a snap. It's the "worse" that causes the problems, because it turns out that there is often quite a bit of "worse." And why should we be expected to put up with it? I think we should change that part of the vow to say, "as long as things are okay." As for the "richer or poorer" and "sickness and health" part, forget about it. Who wants to think about poverty and disease at a time like this? Let's just can that part altogether.

And, finally, there's that terrifying ending, the part that keeps many a man (and no small number of women) away from the altar. It's that " 'til death do you part" part or the more modern "as long as you both shall live." What a bummer! First of all, it reminds the couple at this wonderful, wonderful moment that even if it does last, it doesn't last forever. And it also says, hey, you may be 21 and 19, you may have no idea what you're doing in your life, you may switch careers five times, but right now, today, you are agreeing that you are going to stay with this person for the rest of your (or her or his) life.

Come on! Let's make it more realistic and change it to something like "for three years, subject to renewal," or even "at least until next Thursday."

I know it's probably a fantasy, but I can imagine some day hearing a minister intone, "Do you, Bob, forsaking most others, vow to tolerate Jane, as long as things are okay, or at least until next Thursday?" and "Do you, Jane,...."

[2/25/99]

96

Listen, Pal

Much has been written on the subject of men, women, how different (or similar) we are, and the extent to which differences are due to biology or culture. Some have gone as far as to suggest that we come from different planets, with one author making a huge amount of money from just this thesis. Of course, I'm talking about John Gray, author of *Men are from Mars, Women are from Venus*. I think Gray was on the right track, but in reality I believe men are from Neptune and women are from Pluto. Kids, meanwhile, are from a whole other galaxy.

When sex differences have been studied by scientists who are daring enough to go into this politically charged arena, few differences have withstood the test of rigorous research. Biologically, it seems that we are more similar than we are different. Culture, it appears, does play a great role in shaping us. In some societies, for example, it is men who love to ask directions and women who simply say, "We can find it on our own. I'm not stopping this horse-drawn cart to ask!"

However, there is a difference that appears to be practically universal. In almost every culture, starting at the age of three or four, males are more aggressive than females. Anyone gonna argue with me about this? Come on, come on, just try me!

Now I'm talking here about either direct physical aggression or outright verbal abuse. When it comes to subtle aggression, such as excluding someone from your group and making them feel terrible, females appear to have the edge. This appears to be especially true for younger females, a.k.a. girls. Parents of daughters have told me sad tales of how their daughter was suddenly excluded from a group of friends, and became very upset over this.

This tends not to be boys' style. If a boy is angry at another boy, he simply suggests they "go outside," a term which every male knows means a fight. (It's one of the main reasons I stayed inside pretty much all the time when I was young.) If the second boy agrees to go outside, the two boys fight, with other boys gathered around cheering their favorite on. Sometimes there is even heavy betting on who will win.

After one of the boys has beaten the other one up, they shake hands, and then often go on to become the closest of friends.

Just as every girl grows up fearing boys and men, so too does every boy. In fact, there are many men who will never, under any circumstances, hit a woman. Why should they when there are so many other men they can hit? The reality is -- and men certainly all know this -- the possibility of aggression underlies virtually every male-male interaction.

This can appear subtle to outsiders, i.e., women, because some male-male interactions appear, on the surface, to be friendly, even when it's two strangers interacting. This is due to the fact that a man often uses generic, friendly terms when addressing another man, even one who is a complete stranger. They say things like, "Hey, buddy," or "Hey, pal," even to a man they have never met before.

I practically never do this, but once did try it when I returned to my old neighborhood, where I hadn't been for many years. I went into a gas station, where I knew no one, and called over to one of the guys working there, "Hey, buddy, could you check my oil?" I felt very strange saying it, but the guy didn't bat an eyelash.

But make no mistake. The use of these terms is a thin cover for the basic anger all men feel toward each other. In addition to such terms of endearment as "friend," "pal," etc., men also frequently call each other "man," which seems to establish a kind of male-to-male camaraderie. Yet this too is scant cover for the seething aggression always raging just below the surface.

Consider the following, at least somewhat plausible, conversation:

Two men, essentially strangers to one another, are sitting on a bench waiting for a bus.

Man #1: Hey, man, how ya doin'?
Man #2: Hey, fine, man, fine. What about you?
1: Fine, buddy, just fine.
2: Good, man. So pal, what's new?
1: Not much, buddy, not much.
2: Same here, friend, same here.
1: Some weather we've been having, eh pal?
2: You said it, brother.
1: Listen, friend, could I ask you a favor?
2: Sure thing, pal, you name it.
1: I wonder if you could lend me a few bucks. I'll pay it back quick. Really, my friend.

2: Huh?

1: Buddy, friend, pal, please, some money, not a whole lot.

2: Hey, pal, I'm no bank. Listen, friend, I don't have it, and even if I did...

1. Hey, buddy, you don't have to get all hostile.

2: Oh yeah? Well, just listen, my good friend, you keep up this money stuff, and I'll put you right on your ------' ass!

At this juncture, Man #1 would very likely suggest they "go outside," but, since they already are outside, he may have no recourse but to back off and withdraw into the silence for which men are also famous. Even so, at this point, there is still the possibility of a long and deep friendship developing between these two fun guys.

[3/11/99]

100

The Empty Nest

Sometimes a phrase seems to capture something so perfectly that it becomes a standard part of the language. Even if it becomes a cliché (and what is a cliché anyhow, but a phrase that was originally clever and perfect), it's simply hard to come up with something better. That's the case for "empty nest," the situation that occurs when the youngest of your children leaves the house.

My wife and I have become "empty nesters." Less than a week ago (as I write this), we dropped our youngest child off at college to start his freshman year. Suddenly, for the first time in over 25 years, it is just the two of us at home. That's the problem. The term "empty nest," brilliant as it, is somewhat inaccurate. The nest is not empty. We're still in it. We're still in that same old nest, with all its same old stuff in it. Not only that, when we have to bring out the trash from our nest, we no longer have our strapping 18-year-old with his young back and strong arms to take it out.

What's particularly strange is that even for the last couple of months, our son didn't spend much time in the nest. I don't know why. For some reason that continues to elude me, he seemed to find it more fun to be with his friends than to be with us.

One day I decided to confront him on this.

"I don't get it," I said. "We raised you from babyhood, we know you so well, we'd do anything for you, and yet you prefer to be with your friends than to be here with us. What is it? Have we done something wrong?"

"Later," he said, and he was out the door.

I thought it would be pretty tough for him to say good-bye to us after we had helped him unload his stuff in his dorm room. We thought he would find excuses to have us stay just a little longer. We were sure he would ask us to help him put his stuff away.

This didn't happen. He said, "I'm feeling sort of tired, and I'm getting sweaty. I really want to put my stuff away myself. Maybe you ought to get going."

"Oh, that's okay," my wife said. "We don't mind just hanging out for a little while."

At that point he gazed at us with a look on his face that all parents of teenagers come to know, one that says, It's over. Thanks for the diaper-changing, the games, the kisses and the driving lessons. You did good (of course it should be "you did well," but I'm not going to quibble with the grammar of what someone is thinking), but now it's time for me to...well, it's my turn to...well, what I've got to do now is...PARTY!

Maybe it's different with girls. We have friends who tell us that when they dropped their daughter off at school, she was crying uncontrollably. It was very difficult for them to leave.

My son simply accepted a hug from each of us, said good-bye, and was down the hall to join his new neighbors and soon-to-be friends.

We looked at each other -- which has become one of our primary activities since we dropped our son off -- and realized that the time had come to drive back to the old nest. We could take our time. We could have a leisurely meal at a restaurant on the way back. We could drive below the speed limit. Did it matter?

We are adjusting. But it is, as another empty nester put it recently, "weird." That first night back, the house seemed eerily quiet; ordinarily, a dog barking outside would annoy me, but I yearned for that, for any kind of noise.

Much as my wife and I love each other, we feel sort of lonely. A couple of nights ago, at a local restaurant, we began to talk to a couple next to us that we didn't even know, and realized that perhaps it was time to start "dating" again, not as individuals (God forbid!), but as a couple. That is, we could ask other couples out. We might even be daring, and try to "pick up" another couple.

Suddenly, I remembered a couple we met at a classical musical performance a year or two ago. We had talked for a few minutes, and then the woman -- keep in mind, we'd never met her before -- asked if perhaps we'd like to join them sometime at another concert. We felt very strange. We felt almost as if it were some kind of couples harassment. But now I realize what was probably going on. I'll bet anything that they had recently become empty nesters.

We said no, but if the same thing were to happen today, I'm not sure we could resist.

I'm not saying this empty nest thing is any big deal. So what if the entire pattern of your life has completely changed, if your basic day-to-day dynamic is different, if your fledgling is now 150 miles away, which is much closer than his two siblings. All it takes is a little adjustment. And a couple of trash cans with wheels.

[9/23/99]

103

To Love, Honor And Squabble

Books and articles on marriage and its various problems often point to certain issues as the source of possible discord. These are the biggies, the ones that can tear a couple apart. You don't have to read this stuff to know that some of them are breakdown in communication, differences over spending money, how involved to be with relatives, and how often to have sex.

Now these can be important concerns, no question about it. If a husband says, "I tolerate you, okay?" claiming that this is his way of expressing love, you can see that this couple is going to have problems. Or if she wants both of them to spend every Saturday night with her parents, and he'd rather spend every week-end gambling, this would also not be good. If he wants to have sex every day, and she's the every-other-month type, well, again, it doesn't take a Nostradamus to predict a divorce here.

But these differences and conflicts get all the attention because they are so serious; they do break up marriages. What gets far less attention are the problems couples have who stay married. These are partners who have learned to compromise on the big issues; or one of them has simply given up all attempts at assertiveness. The latter, also known as the "Yes, dear" approach, isn't all that bad, and works well for many couples. But even the "Yes, dear" method won't stop all the little disagreements that can occur when two people attempt what even on the face of it sounds pretty difficult: to live together as long as they are both alive.

As someone who has been married nearly 30 years, I feel qualified to talk about this. And I don't just have my own experience -- as close to perfect as it has been -- to go by; I also have what other long-marrieds have told my wife and me.

To start with, there's snow shoveling. Granted this is only a seasonal problem (and not a problem at all in certain parts of the country), but when snow is a possibility, shoveling presents one of the great challenges to a couple's equanimity. The typical scenario goes like this:

A snowstorm comes and dumps eight inches of snow on the ground. As soon as it has stopped falling, if not before, the husband announces, "Honey, I'm going out to shovel."

"Please," his wife says. "Please don't. You could have a heart attack and die. Let's hire one of the kids on the road to do it."

"What?" he says. "You think I'm too old to do this? Come on! I won't die." He thereupon walks out the door, picks up a shovel, and starts.

After 45 minutes, he comes back in, red and sweaty. On top of this, his back is out.

"My back is out," he announces.

"Great," she says. "That's just great. I told you not to shovel. I knew something like this would happen!"

"No," he says. "You were worried about a heart attack. My heart is fine. I just can't stand up straight."

Another source of discord, one that makes for tension throughout the whole year, is the very serious issue of where people put things. Probably one of the most common questions heard in any marriage is "Honey, why is this here?"

For some reason, exactly where various items are placed on kitchen counters, in cabinets or in the refrigerator, is very important to whomever does the placing. I don't think most of us realize just how habitual are our placing habits. If you open the refrigerator door to find that the milk carton you put on the right side of the shelf is now on the left, well, is that an outrage or what?

What the offended party says isn't anything direct, like "Hey, you moved the milk! I always keep it on the right and now it's on the left. You've ruined my day. Now I'll have to up my Prozac!"

No, marriages last when the aggrieved spouse is more subtle. Hence, the apparently innocent, "Honey, why is this here?"

Not that this doesn't lead to a fight. But at least it's a fight that starts out more gently. Saying "honey" really does help. Long-marrieds have learned that one of the keys to staying together is to call your spouse "honey" or "sweetie" or "love of my life" as often as possible. This helps to reduce the anger your remark is sure to spark.

For example, consider another area of marital conflict: differences in dishwashing style. Those who regularly use a dishwasher can escape this, but for those who don't, there is often a difference in perception as to what constitutes a clean dish. For some people, a dish is not clean unless it is spotless; for others, clean means there may still be a few small dried food particles attached.

When the more fastidious person picks up a dish washed by his or her partner, he or she is tempted to say, "You call this clean?! This is a health hazard! It's disgusting!!" But say that a few times and soon you'll not only be the only one washing dishes, you'll be eating alone and sleeping alone too.

No, the meticulous person who wants to stay married will say, "Oh, sweetie, I know how hard you work, and you did a great job on these dishes, but I think you missed this one little spot, honey."

Yes, there will be a fight. But your marriage will last another day, giving you time for all the other joyful squabbles over driving styles, television preferences, and how high the pile of newspapers should get before someone brings it out for recycling.

[3/9/00]

107

Meeting The Parents

I'm yiping out. In a matter of days, my wife and I will be meeting the parents of our son's fiancée. We've spoken to them on the phone several times, and we did meet her father, very briefly, about five years ago -- soon after our kids started dating -- but we have not yet met her mother.

I don't know why I should be so nervous. What's the big deal here? So what if we're going to be spending two days a thousand miles from home with a couple whose treasure is about to commit herself to spending the rest of her life with our treasure?

Fortunately, our respective treasures will be there too, serving, one could say, as emotional interpreters between two couples who, let's face it, probably would never have met had our children not fallen in love.

Actually, the four of us are better off than a lot of couples in this situation: We really like our daughter-in-law-to-be, and we're pretty sure they feel the same about our son. What's it like when one or both sets of parents are really upset about the choice their child has made, and perhaps with good reason? What kind of small talk goes on then?: "So how long a sentence would Jim have served if he hadn't gotten paroled?" or "Jen says she worked for an 'escort service' for a while. What does that mean, really?"

Still, we are nervous. It's like a blind date that will last 48 hours. Plus it's a reversal of the usual situation where parents worry that their kids won't behave. Now it's our kids who worry that we won't behave.

No question that we're all going to be on our best behavior but, even so, everyone knows that sooner or later someone will say the wrong thing. The fact that we're northerners and they're southerners, and we have very different ethnic, religious, and political backgrounds should make for a really fun couple of days -- as long as no one talks about anything other than sports and the weather.

I want it to go well, I really do. And I am optimistic. Petrified yes, but optimistic. I do recognize the problem here as just one example of the major one we all face as we go through our lives: adjustment.

It never ends, does it? After many years, most of us (often with the help of thousands of hours of therapy) adjust to our parents and who they are or were. Next, we try to adjust to our in-laws, who no doubt find us totally inadequate for their son or daughter. Then, gradually, we adjust to our children, realizing that they are not simply extensions of us but rather separate and independent human beings. Finally, just when we think we can relax, a whole new family is thrown into the mix.

It doesn't help that one hears horror stories from friends whose children have recently married. Terms like "unbearable" and "impossible" are often used to describe the other parents. People wonder, How can it be? Our daughter or son married someone we like so much, so why is it that their parents are so difficult to be with?

I think I have an answer for this. Keep in mind that as children grow up, and especially after they leave their childhood home, they often try very hard not to be like their parents; in fact, they try to be the exact opposite. So if you do really find yourself crazy about your son or daughter's choice of a mate, watch out! Of course, I'm not saying this always happens, and I feel sure that my wife and I will like my son's in-laws-to-be a lot.

It's very important for me to mention, by the way, that this is not the first experience I am having with meeting the new in-laws. My oldest son got married about two years ago, and, in this case, we didn't meet his wife's parents until a couple of days before the wedding. Why, you might ask? Well, it's because she is from Japan, the wedding was in California, and it just hadn't been feasible for us all to get together well before the big day.

It wasn't bad at all. In fact, it actually went quite well. Aside from the excitement of being with people from such a different culture, to celebrate such a wonderful occasion, there was the fact that when you don't understand each other at all, misunderstandings don't happen. All I remember was a great deal of bowing, shaking hands, and smiling. It's really hard to offend someone when they have no idea what you're saying.

But as for what's coming up, yipe!

[5/17/01]

110

"The Look"

A couple of weeks ago, my wife and I were having dinner at a very nice Italian restaurant down in Florida, with a group of about five people, including our son and his soon-to-be in-laws. We had already been with them for over 24 hours, and were getting along well, but still, we were a bit nervous and certainly on our very best behavior.

I was really doing my best, as I had been doing since we started planning for this trip. I had even bought two new and, I must say, rather spiffy shirts for that week-end, one of which I was wearing that night. However, nothing could stop me from doing what I so often do when I eat, namely getting something on my pants or shirt. In this case it was my shirt, and what went on it was some kind of oil.

Uh-oh, I thought, what will my son's in-laws-to-be think of me? How will they feel about their daughter marrying a guy whose dad spills oil on his shirt? So as quickly and inconspicuously as I could, I dipped my napkin in my water and rubbed my shirt with it.

It was at that moment I noticed that my wife, who was seated just to my left, was giving me "the look." We guys all know the look. It's a look that says, "What are you doing (or saying)? How can you embarrass me this way?"

I've been the recipient of the look countless times. In fact, I've come to check to see if I'm getting it whenever I do anything even the least bit out of the ordinary, such as blowing my nose into my napkin (actually, I don't do this, as I know it's grounds for divorce).

There came then a moment of bonding between me and the father of the bride.

"I'm getting the look," I said to him. "Do you know what I mean? Do you ever get the look?"

"Oh yes," he said. "Lots of times."

At that point he did something which immediately endeared him to me. I don't know whether he too had spilled anything on himself, but he also took some of his water and rubbed it on his shirt.

Now we both were getting the look.

I've thought about this little incident a lot in the couple of weeks since it occurred, especially about "the look" and what it means in the grand scheme of things. I think it's a reflection of a basic difference in how women and men feel about their spouses and about the institution of marriage itself. It boils down to this basic paradox:

Women are satisfied with the institution of marriage. They are happy with marriage itself. But they are dissatisfied with their particular husband. They feel that he is less than ideal (often far less) and there must be someone better out there somewhere. With an ideal husband, they feel, marriage would be an ideal state. The look is a wife's way of letting her husband know that he is still falling short.

Men, on the other hand, are generally satisfied

112

with their wives. They can't imagine being married to anyone better. Their wives are fine. It's the institution of marriage they have trouble with. They would love to see a whole lot of different women. But they are perfectly happy with their particular partner. Husbands' looks that bother wives are not disapproving looks at them, but rather appreciative looks at other women.

Each of these other women, in marriages or relationships with a typically deficient man, may fantasize that the guy who is looking at her promises an escape from her own dissatisfactions. Of course, she doesn't realize that he too is, like all men, lacking in social graces not to mention sensitivity and understanding; that, if she were married to him, it wouldn't be long before she was giving him "the look" too.

The look is simply part of what it means to be married. You can see it at all strata of society, even at banquets attended by heads of state and their spouses. Even the most fearsome dictator, whose underlings wouldn't dare to question anything he says or does, knows that if he uses a spoon when he should be using a fork, his wife too is going to give him "the look."

[6/14/01]

113

Sports Talk

One of the many stereotypes of men is that all they like to talk about is sports and women (though not women's sports). We've all seen that scene countless times in movies and sitcoms, where someone says something of great import, like "What are we going to do about Brenda? She's talking about suicide almost every day now," to which a man replies, "So how about those Yankees!"

The reality is that while sports is important for many men, and they do talk about it a lot, there are an almost equal number of men for whom sports is of little interest or importance. Though this research is now about 20 years old, a colleague of mine and I asked a large sample of men how often they talked about sports with male friends, and while 40 percent said "Frequently or often," 37% said "Never or rarely" (the rest fell in between). For women the figures then were 15 and 71 percent, respectively, though these numbers might be very different today, especially given the rise of women's sports. (Nonetheless, I can't imagine a woman responding to a comment about a person's despondency by saying, "How about the New York Liberty!")

Since, by training, I am a psychologist, and thus doomed never to allow anything people do just be something I notice and acknowledge, but rather something I think about and analyze, I have thought about the role that talking about sports has for men. Women often say it's a way for men to avoid tender feelings, but that doesn't make sense to me. We have so many ways to avoid those kind of feelings, from drugs and alcohol to rage and violence. Why would we need to talk about a pitcher's earned run average?

Another related view is that men use sports talk to avoid talking about themselves. I don't think this is the answer either. True, a great many guys do talk about sports a lot, but they know when it's appropriate. When was the last time you heard a conversation that went like this?:

Mike: So Jim, how do you feel about your new job? Is it what you hoped it would be?

Jim: Well, Clemens record is 7 and 1, but his ERA is 4.00. Maddux is definitely having a better season. I know he's lost 5 games, but his ERA is 2.43.

Another theory holds that men use sports talk as a way to exclude women. This is absurd. It's like saying women talk about menstruation and clothes as a way to exclude men. Men have all kinds of other ways to exclude women, including many disgusting habits, which I will spare the reader. Besides, more and more women are interested in sports these days; indeed Susan Waldman is a highly respected sports commentator and announcer on New York radio and television.

A theory with strong support is that discussing sports has long been a bond between fathers and sons. Again, today's generation of fathers can enjoy talking about it with their daughters too; but when I was growing up, sports was primarily something that boys were interested in. And it was a place where fathers could communicate with their sons in a way that was both comfortable and exciting. This isn't to say that women relatives were excluded. In fact, I went to my first night baseball game (at wonderful Ebbets Field in Brooklyn) with my Aunt Ida. But my Aunt Ida was also into hugging, making great meals and listening when I told her of my concerns about life. My father was into my grades in school, whether or not I hit back when another kid hit me, and the Yankees. When I went to a Yankee game with him, I didn't have to worry about how I was doing; we both could worry about how they were doing (which, in the '50s, usually was great).

Some conjecture that sports, both watching and playing, is a way for people to get out their aggressions in a non-lethal way. Playing sports is often violent, but sports deaths are generally rare. Sports talk is rarely even violent. However, by its very nature, sports is competitive, often highly so, and competition and aggression often go together, like cholesterol and atherosclerosis.

Other theories as to why people -- still, I suspect, mostly men -- talk about sports so much are also intriguing. For example, there is the notion that most of life is so boring, what else can we talk about? Then there is the hypothesis that we talk about sports a lot because, in today's technological world, it's the last hold-out of humans as physical beings. Yes, playing a sport well definitely requires intelligence, but the most brilliant person in the world isn't going to get to the pros if he or she isn't incredibly gifted physically. The aunt of a fine NBA player told me that his athletic skills first became evident when he was successfully catching fly balls in the outfield when he was four years old.

Almost none of us could do this as children, nor can our own children do it, but it's fun to talk about. It's kind of a relief after hearing how this or that friend's kid just got on the honor roll for the 14th straight semester.

Finally, there is the utterly crazy theory that people talk about sports because it can be exciting, unpredictable, beautiful to watch, interesting, and ever-changing.

Yeah, but who's gonna really believe that?

[6/28/01]

Perfect People

Some years ago, my wife and I were at the home of friends, along with another couple. We and the other couple were telling the usual stories of our ungrateful teen-age children, who, after all we did for them, didn't care to spend one more minute than was absolutely necessary with us; told us -- sometimes not so gently -- that we were losing it; and seemed uncomfortable bordering on claustrophobic when we tried to hug them.

Suddenly, one of the children of the host couple arrived home from college unexpectedly. You would have thought it was the arrival of the team from the Publishers' Clearinghouse Sweepstakes delivering a check for a million dollars, or that the son hadn't been home in many years -- rather than the several weeks it had actually been. His mother screamed with delight, they embraced each other warmly, and she went on for at least a minute or two on how wonderful it was that he had come home.

We and the other couple just sat there. We didn't say anything, but I was pretty sure we were all thinking the same thing: Look at this. We can't match this. We are, at best, inadequate parents, who surely wouldn't greet our child that way. In fact, we'd consider it a good start if we could say something more loving than "What are you doing home?"

Being in that house at that moment let me have

a taste of how it must feel to be on an American League team other than the Yankees. This mother was perfect. It wasn't just the way she greeted her son that told us that, it was everything she said about him and his sisters. It wasn't that she bragged about her children; it was that she accepted them, fully and completely.

Most people you run into have obvious flaws or concerns. Sometimes they'll tell you about them (they might say, "I'm obsessed by Scrabble. The only time I'm happy is when I'm playing Scrabble, and nothing else seems to mean anything to me anymore."); sometimes you'll notice them on your own, after a little while, or after months or years. But there are a handful of people who just seem to do things right. They are the perfect people, and I hate them. I don't mean I hate them like I wish them harm or never want to see them again. I mean I hate the fact that by their very existence they cause me to question everything I do.

Sometimes people like this brag. But you don't have to be a psychologist to know that this means that all may not be perfect in their lives. It's a given in psychology that whenever someone keeps telling you how wonderful everything is for them or their children, it means that deep down they are miserable. Or at least, that's what those of us who are openly dissatisfied with our lives would like to think.

But whether they brag or not, perfect people are really annoying. After a while, you realize that what you really want to hear from them is how something went wrong. Nothing big. You don't want to hear that anyone is sick or that one of their kids is strung out on drugs. You just want to hear that Ms. Dean's List flunked a course.

It's very hard to be friends with someone for whom everything just seems to go so smoothly. You find yourself constantly saying, "Oh, that's great." or "Really? Your teen-age daughter told you you're the best mother in the world?! That's wonderful," when what you really want to say is, "Leave me alone," or "Oh yeah? Well, after a few more years of global warming, we'll *all* be toast."

You would think, given how hard it is for you to be friends with a perfect person, that he or she would have trouble making friends, but even there you are denied the pleasure of another's inadequacy. Perfect people seem to have lots of friends, which is just what you should expect, since they give great parties, at which the food, drink and company are, well, perfect.

But don't let appearances fool you. Yes, their homes may be full of good-looking, well-dressed, well-to-do people who are smiling, laughing and seem to be having a good time. But it's all a sham. They miss what the rest of us have -- the joys, fun and fellowship of the frustrated and discontent.

[3/7/02]

TheraDate

Usually my unsolicited mail is boring and not even worth the few minutes I spend on it before making the decision to recycle it. But every once in a while something comes along that really does catch my attention. So it was a few days ago, when I received a one-page flyer from "TheraDate."

I received this mailing because I am a licensed psychologist (a list of which the TheraDate people had used for their mass mailing).

Yes, that's right, I am licensed by the state of New York to practice psychology, and as far as the TheraDate people know, I do. Actually, I don't.

So what is TheraDate? It is essentially a matchmaking service for people in therapy. To quote the flyer, "We are a group of mental health professionals of all major disciplines who realized we couldn't introduce *our patients to our own patients*. We can, however, introduce our or your patients to *each other's* patients." (their italics).

The rationale is that people in therapy are "interested in their own behaviors and how their behaviors might impact others." Sounds good, but -- and I am sorry if this comes as a shock to my regular readers -- I have been in therapy, and while it's true that I am interested in my own behavior and how it impacts others, that is not the main reason I have seen therapists. The main reason is that I suffer from difficulties ranging from minor compulsions (such as checking the coffeepot three or four times to make sure it's unplugged before I go out) to more significant concerns (such as a fear of failure and fear of success).

I would guess this is true of other people who are in or have had therapy. I am not putting down such people, being one of them myself. But I suspect the dream of every client (a term I much prefer to TheraDate's "patient") is to marry "up," as it were, to marry someone who actually doesn't need therapy. To my everlasting joy, I met and married such a person more than 30 years ago.

Nonetheless, intrigued by the one-page advertisement, I decided to go on their website, which has several pages for clients (and a few for therapists). I primarily wanted to see what the client would see if he or she were interested.

The home page starts out with the words, "You are an intelligent, verbal, achievement-oriented person using therapy to improve your life." Wow! I like that. Forget the therapy part. I love having anyone tell me I'm intelligent, verbal and achievement-oriented -- even if they've never met me.

It goes on to say that TheraDate's team of therapists will help me find someone like me, who, most importantly, is smart enough also to be in therapy (you're also eligible if you've been discharged from therapy less than two years ago).

How it works is that I register, and give TheraDate's team of mental health professionals the name and phone number of my therapist, who will then fill out a questionnaire to send back to TheraDate. The rationale here vs. computer match-up schemes is that your therapist will be more honest about you than you will be about yourself. You probably wouldn't want a prospective partner to know that you tend to have hourly mood swings, but your therapist may point that out.

Of course, once word of TheraDate really gets out, new clients will have more reason than ever not to be honest in their therapy sessions. If I know that in a couple of months (the minimum time in therapy you need for TheraDate) I'll be asking my shrink to send in information on me, I'm not going to tell him or her that I was inconsolable for months after my pet piranha died. Rather I'll say that one of my biggest problems in life is that I can't stand the way other men talk about women in such a sexist way. My appreciation and love of women -- especially beautiful, misunderstood ones -- is so strong that it sometimes gets in the way of whatever machismo feelings I might otherwise have.

In case you're wondering, the message for therapists is that patients being actively treated for drug, alcohol or violence problems be told that they are not eligible for TheraDate. I don't know. I'd hate to be a therapist seeing a big, violent, drug-addicted client who says to me one day, "Hey, I heard about this thing called TheraDate. How about signing me up!"

Actually, one thing that you are guaranteed in TheraDate is that you will be meeting people who are doing well financially, or at least were before they signed up. The fee is $2,000 for the first year. Sounds like it might be a tough one to get your health insurance to pay for too.

Finally, let's say it works. You meet Ms., Mr., or even Dr. Right. It goes well. You find that you have complementary neuroses. You're manic, she's depressed. You're obsessive, he's lackadaisical. You both love children's cartoons. So you wind up getting married. It's terrific.

But what do you say when someone -- and it could be one of your children -- asks you how you met? Do you make something up? Do you have a story? Or do you tell the truth?

I guess that would be something to talk about in therapy.

[4/4/02]

I Love You, But You're Impossible!

One of the great paradoxes of life is that conflict occurs most frequently between people who love each other: Husbands and wives, parents and children, siblings and siblings. It is in these relationships that we are most likely to find people fighting.

I am going to focus here on marriage, spending a little time on why couples fight, and then making a few suggestions as to how they might avoid having these fights escalate into all-out marital warfare. I'm not going to show this to my wife, because she'll probably criticize what I've written, since she doesn't really appreciate me, even after all I've done for her!

Anyhow, why do husbands and wives fight, and what can they do about it?

First off, they fight because, whether or not men are truly from Mars and women from Venus, or that was just a cute metaphor to sell millions of books, the fact is that men and women are different. We don't understand each other, we never will understand each other, and no matter how hard we try not to, we will inevitably say the wrong thing. There is a theory that the fault here lies mainly with men, and some men guiltily go along with this.

Not me. The other day I was talking to a woman

I know and like, and she said, referring not just to her own husband, but to men in general, "Men are babies."

"Babies?!" I cried out. "Why do you say that? Why? Why? We're not babies, we're not, we're not!"

She smiled.

"See what I mean?" she said.

Men are also accused of being insensitive, of not noticing the nonverbal cues to how their wives are feeling. An almost sure fight-starter for many couples is the husband actually believing his wife is feeling good when he asks her how she's doing and she says, "Fine."

But women have their own issues. Woe to the man who doesn't quickly realize that for the vast majority of women, the most important thing in their lives -- aside from their children -- is how they look. And, while in most aspects of marriage honesty is the best policy, here is a place where there is only one answer to a question. When he hears "How do I look?" a man should reflexively say, "Great." Blind men should say it.

There are many other issues that lead to marital fights, but my wife says I tend to go on too long when I discuss anything, so I'll just leave it at those three for now. But as I promised earlier, I'll now provide some ways to manage the inevitable conflicts.

That's right, fights are going to happen. It's how you manage them that will determine whether or not your marriage lasts. Here are three simple suggestions to keep fights under control:

1. Use "I" statements rather than "you" statements. Psychologists and marital counselors agree that putting the focus on *your* feelings rather than your

partner's inadequacies will go a long way to keeping fights manageable.

Example: *Don't* say, "You're an idiot!"
Do say, "I think you're an idiot!"

2. Schedule your fights. It seems natural to fight when you're angry, like right after your spouse tells you that he has quit his job to become a professional gambler. But beware. Words said in the heat of anger can do lasting damage. So bite your tongue, and as soon as the bleeding stops, say, "Let's talk about this soon, okay? How does next Tuesday morning at my lawyer's office sound?"

3. Apologize, apologize, apologize. When in doubt, say you're sorry. If your partner says, "You don't have to apologize," then apologize for the apology!

You're married. The chances are that sometime in the last hour you did or said the wrong thing, so go ahead, say you're sorry. Keep this in mind: It's better to apologize ten times when you don't have to than *not* to apologize once when you do. Why take chances?

[9/19/02]

127

Ah, Love!

"Love comforteth like sunshine after rain."

--William Shakespeare

"Love is a portion of the soul itself, and it is of the same nature as the celestial breathing of the atmosphere of paradise."

--Victor Hugo

"Love stinks."

--J. Geils Band

"Love can be so boring."

--Vertical Horizon

Ah, love! Just a little four-letter word about which poets, playwrights and novelists have written for centuries. Great writers have shown us that there is nothing quite like love for raising us into ethereal emotional realms.

Yes, but in the last 50 years or so, who has come closest to capturing how people really feel? Who talks to us on our car radios and TVs, in supermarkets, in restaurants and on our computers? Songwriters and singers, that's who, and what they have to say touches us in a very direct way. They show us what we really don't want to face: that times have changed and with that, so has what we mean by love.

I know, Shakespeare was a wonderful writer, but still, keep in mind that he lived more than four centuries ago, when love was pretty much all you had to give you any fun at all. After all, back in the 16th century, there was no central heating or indoor plumbing. Life was hard. Worst of all, there was no television. So what could people do to distract themselves? Put more coal in the stove? Watch another execution?

Furthermore, in those days, with life expectancies being what they were, you generally didn't have to worry about long-term commitments, so saying "I love you" took a lot less courage. The idea of spending the rest of your life with someone doesn't sound all that bad when it means maybe 10 years, 15 at the most.

Obviously, the Supremes' famous words, "You can't hurry love" would have been totally inappropriate in Shakespeare's time.

Things were a bit better by the time Victor Hugo came along in the 19th century. But still it wasn't all peaches and cream. After all, how great could things be to inspire a novel called *Les Misérables*?

Even as late as 1966, when the Supremes sang that line, love still had a certain aura about it. True, the feelings about love were not as wondrously positive as they were in 1955, when "Love is a Many Splendored Thing" hit the charts, but at least there still seemed to be some hope for this most central of human emotions.

However, by 1980, with the divorce rate soaring, and men and women clueless about how to get along with each other, the J. Geils band finally said what everyone feels at some point in his or her life: "Love stinks." No, it's not the message we want to give our children, and it's not what we'd want to hear at our wedding or theirs (Adam Sandler's rendition of it in "The Wedding Singer" notwithstanding); but it does serve as a good counterbalance to the flowery words about love that people continue to write, primarily in the text of Hallmark cards.

Finally, in the '90s, with MTV, video games and an Internet with anything you want available at the click of a mouse, it took a bold band to say what so many of us had been secretly thinking: As compared to all this technological fun, "love can be so boring."

Now lest I get letters from lovestruck young people, or older people who have been married for many years and still find their partners irresistibly fun to be with -- which includes me, of course -- let me say that I'm just making a social observation. No doubt, couples fought in Shakespeare's time too, and not all of his quotes are sweetness and light either (consider "The course of true love never did run smooth"). But with adequate heating hard to come by, and physical existence itself a major struggle, few people had the time or energy to criticize what was, at the time, pretty much the only reason to get up in the morning.

We should be grateful to live in a time when the plethora of pleasures all around us makes love something at which we can poke fun. We've got CDs, DVDs and SUVs. So, as the band Tank sang so presciently in their 1982 album, *Filth Hounds of Hades*, "Who needs love songs?"

[2/6/03]

130

True Intimacy

Books and articles on friendship, marriage and mental health often talk about the importance of intimacy. They are not talking about physical intimacy, of course, which is generally there by definition in the most intimate of relationships, but rather the willingness to share one's innermost feelings. When I looked up "intimate" in my thesaurus, it gave me words like "confidential," "private," and "secret."

Men, whose gender is now blamed for all the problems in the world, are most frequently accused of being afraid of intimacy. As a man, I take offense at this. Of course, I'm not going to share with you the deep-seated reasons for my reactions, because, after all, I am a man. But I would argue that if we look at what *real* intimacy is, I think men are certainly into it.

Male or female, you have to be into it in order to stay in a long-term relationship with someone. Because I maintain that true intimacy isn't sharing your innermost feelings with someone. It's experiencing another person's various bodily functions and not leaving!

(If you think I'm off the wall on this, just check out the line of Carlton greeting cards, in which the most personal noises and behaviors are the main subject matter.)

The things long-married partners -- yeah, and it's

probably men more than women -- do in each other's presence would end almost any dating relationship. I'm not saying these things add to marital bliss, but they certainly are a sign of intimacy.

In fact, paradoxically, the very things that turn us off about our significant other are the signs that he or she feels comfortable with us. An insightful woman of my acquaintance, who has been married for about 18 years, said that she realized one day that the only reason she found so many things about her husband to be annoying was that she knew him so well. She realized that she'd feel the same about any other guy she knew as well.

I stifled a burp and said, "Yes, I think you're right."

During dating and courtship we are so careful about what we say and do. In fact, many of us have to drink a lot even to begin to free ourselves to be ourselves. This does lead to a certain kind of intimacy, of course, as captured in the Latin expression, *in vino veritas*: in wine there is truth. But in a good long-term relationship, eventually we may not need intoxicants to free ourselves up to say and do the things that would cause anyone but our partner to head for the hills.

Another sign of intimacy, though a more positive one, is the use of pet names. I'm not talking about the ones we all use, like "honey," "sweetie," and "muffinhead." I'm talking about the very special ones, the really silly-sounding ones that we wouldn't tell anyone else even under torture. This is real intimacy -- being able to call someone "poogie-woogie," and not having them throw up or walk out.

When we think of the ultimate in intimate

relationships, we tend to think of long-term partners, who often happen to be husbands and wives. But many a man has come to realize that while he may think of his wife as his best friend, he can't talk to her the way he talks to his best *male* friend. He often learns this the hard way when, sitting with his wife of many years, he sees a very attractive young woman walk by, and says, without thinking, "Wow, look at her!"

This is not intimacy; this is stupidity.

Even when it's something that is exciting, something you can't wait to tell people, be careful about sharing it with your spouse. I knew a man who, some 15 years ago, happened to see the young Mariel Hemingway in Central Park. He came back to his apartment and excitedly told his wife, "I just saw Mariel Hemingway and she is incredibly beautiful!"

To his surprise, his wife didn't share his enthusiasm about his encounter with the okay-looking (you see that, honey?) Ms. Hemingway.

He hadn't been married all that long, and I believe his marriage survived his verbal indiscretion. But his experience shows that even with our partner, our lover, our soulmate, we still have to watch what we say. That's why God made good friends.

True, it takes a very special friend to stick around when you do those Carlton card types of things, but at least you can let your hair down when you talk about someone's attractiveness.

But always remember whom you're talking to. It will take years to live it down if you forget and call your best friend "Mooshiepoo."

[3/6/03]

About the Author

At a time when success demands expertise in one area and singularity of purpose, when the term "Renaissance man" is hundreds of years out of date, Mark Sherman has remained committed to the notion that it's better to do a bunch of different things well and get nowhere than do one thing extraordinarily well and achieve fame and/or fortune.

Starting out as a math major in college, he went on to receive a PhD in psychology from Harvard in 1969. Since that time, he has (1) taught psychology for over 25 years, (2) coauthored a trade book in the field, (3) written and performed on numerous occasions his mostly humorous songs, (4) served on his community's town board, and (5) written a bi-weekly humor column for more than 19 years.

Sherman is married and the father of three grown children. He lives in New Paltz, New York with his wife, Shelley, and no animals.